FIGHTER

ANDY LEE
with Niall Kelly

Gill Books
Hume Avenue
Park West
Dublin 12
www.gillbooks.ie

Gill Books is an imprint of M.H. Gill & Co.

© Andy Lee 2018, 2019
First published in hardback 2018
First published in paperback 2019
978 07171 8489 7

Print origination by Carole Lynch
Copy-edited by Susan McKeever
Proofread by Emma Dunne
Printed by Clays Ltd, Bungay, Suffolk

This book is typeset in 13.5pt Minion
Title and chapter headings in Frutiger Light

The paper used in this book comes from the wood pulp of managed forests. For every tree felled, at least one tree is planted, thereby renewing natural resources.

5 4 3 2

Andy Lee was the WBO middleweight world champion from 2014 to 2015, making him the first Irish boxer to win a world title on American soil since 1934. Having boxed with Repton Boxing Club in London from the age of eight, upon his family's return to Ireland, Lee joined St Francis ABC in Limerick and went on to represent Ireland at the Olympics in 2004. He signed his first professional contract with Emanuel Steward in 2005 and moved to Detroit to train in the world-renowned Kronk Gym until Steward died in 2012, after which Lee joined up with English trainer Adam Booth. Andy retired in February 2018 and lives in Dublin with his wife and daughter.

Niall Kelly is a journalist with The42.ie. He ghost-wrote Philly McMahon's autobiography, *The Choice*, which was the BGE Irish Book Awards and eir Sports Book of the Year in 2017.

'La mort n'est rien; mais vivre vaincu et sans gloire,
c'est mourir tous les jours.'
('Death is nothing; but to live defeated and
without glory is to die every day.')
– Napoléon Bonaparte (1769–1821)

For Maud and Julia

‹ ›

Fighting is a natural thing. But professional fights, prize fights, twelve rounds of championship boxing bound by the Queensberry Rules, any sort of rules, those types of fights are unnatural. They're packages of planning and promotion and pomp and ceremony; they're stage shows, some small and some big and some worthy of any of the great residencies that have gone before in the hotels and casinos of Las Vegas. Like the fight down the lane ten minutes after the school bell sounds for the final time of the day, it has to be engineered into place not only to make sure that the chosen two, willing or otherwise, uphold the first part of their end of the bargain by showing up at the right time and the right place, but also to guarantee that they have a crowd, a bullring, an amphitheatre, a coalition of eyes that lend the whole scene its legitimacy and ensure that the second part of the bargain, the violence itself – sometimes tame, rarely skilled, and often brutally frenzied – follows as agreed, because what is the point of this type of fight if there is nobody there to watch it and whoop and cheer and bay? But a real fight doesn't demand an audience. It isn't trailed neatly by a prelude of trash talk and exaggerated storylines. It happens in an instant, a reflex action as old as human nature itself. Fight over flight as the only response because someone has injured you or hurt you or upset you in some way, and the only retribution that can bring you any compensation or consolation is a physical one. That kind of fight in its most pure, raw, unconstrained, maniacal form – not brought to you by Bob Arum's Top Rank Incorporated in association with DiBella Entertainment, not sponsored by *Tecate con carácter* or sanctioned by the Nevada State Athletic Commission along with the World Boxing Organisation with its referee and its three scoring judges at ringside from Nevada, Nevada and Connecticut. A fight without the interminable build-up, the lights, the TV cameras, the posters and packed arenas and purses worth a million dollars or none – that fight is inherently natural. Sometimes it's instinctive, from the slightest spark to fully ablaze in an instant, and sometimes it's premeditated, bubbling, festering, waiting for its moment of maximum impact, but it's always driven by emotion. Well, nearly always. It can happen at any time or in any place, because total strangers fight and best friends fight and sworn enemies fight and families fight, and the fallout can rarely be predicted and the consequences are rarely the same, because some fights are easy to mend and move on from, but some fights endure and worry at the loose threads of what remains of a relationship for evermore. But for two men to meet and sign contracts to fight and arrange a time and date maybe eight, ten or twelve weeks in the future, and then hold a press conference to try and help sell tickets, it's unnatural. It's absurd. Where is the emotion? Where is the instinctive response that you didn't even know you possessed until it has already overcome you and drawn you into the first dice roll of a physical confrontation that until that split second only existed in your thoughts and your imagination? That's not how it works, because when two fighters agree to fight it's not personal, or at least most of the time it's not, but that doesn't mean that there's nothing at stake. No, quite the opposite. For some fighters everything is at stake: sums of money that can change a life and sums that would barely sustain a life until next Saturday night and the next small hall. Your health prized away as collateral every time you step through those ropes. Your reputation too – it's all on the line. So just because there's nothing personal doesn't mean that there's no anticipation, and once that date is set it takes up residency at the forefront of your mind. It becomes the reference point through which all time and events are now understood. Everything in your life moves towards that date. Every decision you make every day is to benefit you on that date. Every pad you hit. Every meal you eat. It all trickles down to one moment in time when the talking is over and the seconds are out and the crowd has transformed into a wall of white noise. That's the moment when you need to be at your mental and physical peak. It's understandable that the date occupies a permanent space in your thoughts, and it might expand or it might contract, but it will never totally disappear. It's always there. Even when the fight is over and your hand is raised or left limp by the referee's side, it will still be there. Because once a fight happens it exists forever. Duran and Leonard on 25 November 1980. Hagler and Hearns on 15 April 1985. Every time you look at your professional boxing record from now until the day you die the fight will be there, and it will be a part of history, and it will be a part of you. No matter how much you wish you could have that moment again to throw a punch or take one back, you never will. You have to live with the consequences, tied to your name and tied to your identity in neat and tidy numbers, the messy reality obscured by each one: pain, sweat, sacrifice, incomparable happiness and utter devastation that no single digit can ever encompass. The accumulation of those digits over the course of a career can't paint your picture in anything more than the broadest brushstrokes, and yet it's the first thing that people ask you. What do you do? I'm a boxer. What's your record? And when they learn the answer, no matter how big the first number might be, everyone's thoughts are instinctively drawn to the second, because one of the small cruelties of human nature dictates that you might have been a world champion once upon a time, but people will inevitably ask you about the night you lost your belt, not the night you won it. Even with a fighter like the great Rocky Marciano, who never knew what it was like to be confronted with his defeats as he walked down the street or grabbed a quick coffee or ate his dinner, even with a legend like that, it's the impenetrable zero that people fixate on, not the many heroic deeds that it took to construct the forty-nine. So when all of the hard work is done and the date is near, your body knows that its time has come again. If you're lucky, the rhythm of your days matches the rhythm of fight night: when you wake, when you sleep, when you eat, when you go to the toilet. Then you go to this place where you agreed to be at the time you agreed to be there, to stand opposite the man you said you would fight. And the bell rings.

‹ ›

Darryl Cunningham is only on his feet for seventy-seven seconds, off his feet for ten, and then his night is over as quickly as it started.

It's late on a Wednesday and outside the front door of B.B. King's Blues Club and Grill, Times Square hums to its usual oblivious tune of engines idling, tourists snapping their cameras into the bright lights, and street artists hustling to make a dollar.

The room has slowly filled over the course of the last few hours so that by the time Cunningham slumps, defeated, to bring a premature end to our main event, it's standing room only with people wedged in around the bar at the back. If the light is right, you can almost read the labels of the whiskey bottles sitting on the top shelf, likely to be untouched on a night like tonight. It's a small room, and even when it's at capacity, your audience might be six or seven hundred people, tops, certainly no more than a thousand at its absolute limit.

This is where you go when you lose. Let me out of here and in ten minutes I could be at Madison Square Garden, although when I got there I'd be standing outside its locked doors with the rest of the world. Inside is reserved for the greats of history, for winners, and for those who are still on the cusp of their ultimate victory and clinging onto the hope that they might one day prove themselves worthy. Those living, breathing museums of boxing are no place for a fighter who has slipped out of the headlines and into the shadows, into that purgatory where there's a question mark over whether or not you can truly be considered a title contender anymore and a thinly veiled wonder if you ever deserved to be a part of the conversation in the first place.

But there'll always be a spot in B.B. King's. I can let my ego tell me that a night like this is beneath me; that even if Cunningham's record, with his twenty-eight wins and four losses, looks similar on paper to my own 29–2, we live in two different worlds. But in reality, it's not so clear. I can remind myself that I am a world title contender, that this time a year ago I was getting ready for the biggest fight of my life, my shot, but a year is a long time in boxing and so much has changed.

New life, new home, new coach. No belt.

Why am I here? There are a lot of reasons, but mainly, I'm here because I lost to Julio César Chávez Junior, the WBC middleweight champion of the world. I'm here because I have a new coach and the only way that we'll ever get to know each other is by working together and training. He's not here with me tonight, but I might as well take whatever fights I am being offered and see if I can take all of our hours of talk and tactics out of the gym, put them into action in the ring, and make a few quid at the same time. And I'm here because when my star was on the rise, which was not that long ago, my promoter signed me to a new deal which guaranteed me a certain number of fights, and now he's upholding his end of the bargain, although not in the circumstances that either of us had imagined.

This business is ruthless and it's frightening how quickly you can be forgotten. Even if you haven't been forgotten, it can certainly feel that way.

I've been convincing myself that I didn't need a difficult fight tonight, that I've nothing to prove, that my credentials are still sound, and that patience will be my best friend if I can just sit tight and wait, keep doing what I'm doing until the next opportunity comes. And it will come.

As well as that, my wedding day is only a few weeks away, and there's only so much damage this guy can do in a minute and a half if he even manages to lay a meaningful glove on me in such a narrow window. Soon I'll be married, and it's more than just a word, or a ring on the finger, or a big day out with our friends and family. In one way, nothing changes, and at the same time everything does. I owe it to Maud to make the best decisions for us, for our little family that's just the two of us for now but maybe, hopefully, some day will be more. How much longer can I keep fighting the Darryl Cunninghams of the world for bad money on bad cards that nobody is watching? How much longer can I keep selfishly telling myself that I am still going to be a world champion when all of the evidence is laughing at me in the face?

I know Cunningham. I know him from Detroit. He's a decent fighter, and he has that Detroit state of mind where he wants to be the King of the City, the guardian at the gates, putting the up-and-comers and the wannabes in their place, taking the adulation and applause, the tips of the cap as he walks down the street, cultivating this reputation as a man to be feared and respected. You don't want to fight Darryl Cunningham; he's a hard bastard.

But when you take guys like him out of Detroit, when you step them up and out of their comfort zone and force them to face a fighter with some pedigree, the fish is moved from his little pond to the big, bad ocean and now he's floundering. Nobody knows who Darryl Cunningham is in New York City, they've never heard his name or wanted to shake his hand, and he knows it. He knows that his reputation counts for nothing here and that I'm certainly not bothered by it. I saw that the moment he shook my hand at the weigh-in yesterday – meek, deferential, humbling himself a little so that he could try to make some sort of friendly overture, a first plea for mercy as we stepped off the scales.

I try him early with a couple of jabs to the body, nothing with too much meat, just little testers, but he's withering already and I know that this won't take long. Roger, my brother, yells at me from the corner, although he hardly needs to raise his voice in a place like this.

'You see it, you see it, right? You see it.'

I had seen it, the space to step into for the kill. I feint for the body, and as he covers up again, I whip my fist up and away until it slams into the place where the hard part of his jaw and the soft skin meet, an uppercut and a hook all in one.

And I know, as I let my hands go and I land that final flurry of punches and Cunningham falls at my feet, I know that back home in Ireland the news of my thirtieth professional victory will barely register, nothing more than a convenient space-filler along the side of whatever happens to be the main story of the day.

Outside on Times Square, life goes on.

LIMERICK

‹ ›

As a kid, I never wanted to be a world champion.

My runner slips on the concrete as I try to force my hand through the final few inches so that the glove fits snugly. A small circle has already formed outside our family's trailer in London.

'Can I be Rocky?'

'You were Rocky the last time. You have to be Creed this time. Or you can be the Russian.'

'I don't like Creed or the Russian. I want to be Rocky.'

I always found this a bit of a dilemma before I was old enough to even appreciate what the word meant: it's hard to pretend to be somebody when your heart is not in it, but at the same time, you still don't really want to get punched in the face.

If you had to fight one of the Lee brothers, I was the one that you wanted to be in against when the spaces between the twenty or so trailers and caravans that made up the Bow Triangle transformed into our Caesar's Palace for an hour, or for however long it took for one of us to accidentally end up with a black eye or the first signs of a bloodied nose to start trickling down towards the upper lip. If you took one look at me between the ages of seven and twelve, you'd have fancied your chances. I was short and I was heavy; I wasn't a boxer, but I was a fighter.

My eyes are filling as my brother Ned catches me cleanly again, not in the slightest bit concerned about the six-year age advantage that he holds over me; man against boy, in every sense. I blink the tears away as quickly as I can. I don't want anybody to notice, even though they've all seen me cry before, and I want to be able to see his next shot so that I can get out of its way. Too late.

I keep walking forward, trying to keep Ned honest with punches of my own but taking each of his in return. I paw at my own face, like a boxer, wiping away whatever evidence there is of this latest hiding before any fresh marks can accumulate.

'Stop that. Ned! What are you doing? Leave the child alone and put the gloves away.'

My mam, Ann, hears the commotion – the ooohs and the aaahs of our friends that have gathered around to watch – and leans her head out of the caravan to ring the final bell for today; Ned wins on points by a distance as per usual, but I was so stubborn, I would never quit.

When I fought Ned it was always the main event – not because it was the fight that everyone wanted to see, but because when we were done, that would be the fighting over for the day. There might be a group of ten or twenty hanging around the trailers on any given afternoon and we'd close over the gate and everyone would have their go, sparring against each other, sparring against us, but most days it would wind up with me taking a bit of a schooling at Ned's hands, and that would be the end of it all.

I was thirteen, maybe fourteen, the last time that we fought. Ned had just got married, and a lot of our family and friends were still around. It was his idea.

'Come on, Andy, let's put on the gloves and we'll give it a go for a few minutes.'

There's a tiny bit of hesitation, from me rather than from him. It's been a while since he's boxed properly or even trained; not that he's gotten out of shape, or anything like that, nor has the hard-wired talent that made him one of the best amateurs in London, in the UK, for years suddenly short-circuited. I'm still a stubby little fighter, but Repton Boxing Club is like a second home to me at this stage, and I'm down there more nights of the week than I'm not. I'm fitter and stronger than the nine-year-old that he was able to boss around at will but maybe he doesn't realise that.

Maybe he does because, after all, it's still a man in his early twenties fighting against a teenager. Even on my best day, I still wouldn't beat him but the first time we trade, maybe the second, he knows the gap is closing. I'm putting it up to him. He knows I'm coming.

'Ah, that'll do you now, take the gloves off there.'

Mushy, my eldest brother – his name is Tommy but we all call him Mushy – was a very good fighter when he was growing up, but Ned was a boxer in the truest sense of the word. The letters kept coming to the site, even after he'd given up, trying to coax him into camps for the English national team in the hope that he would try to qualify for the 2000 Olympics in Sydney. He was gone from boxing at that stage though and he never went back.

There was another letter:

A winner never quits and a quitter never wins.
Best of luck, Ned,
Reggie Kray

———

I want to be like Ned and like Mushy. We go to watch them box in York Hall, or sometimes at the weekend, we'll squeeze into the back of the car, elbows and knees stacked like a game of Tetris, and we'll drive out of London, to Kent or somewhere, to watch them box in a little hall where everything inside is coloured different shades of brown and it smells a bit like old cigarettes. Ned and Mushy always win.

I don't know anything about Repton, except that it's the place where they go to train and that's a cool thing that they're very proud to tell people.

'I'm a boxer. I box for Repton.'

Repton is where the good boxers go, they tell me as they put pads on their hands and get me to hit them as hard as I can. Don't move your feet. Keep your arm straight. Hit me. Good. Again. Hit me harder. Repton is for champions, they tell me. Repton is for winners. When you're a little bit bigger and you start training, you'll go to Repton.

Sometimes my dad, Tom, goes down to the club to watch Ned and Mushy train, and I'm allowed to go with him. There must be a lot of champions and winners because all of their posters and photographs are stuck to the wall, so many that you can't even see if the yellow paint has peeled away or count the white tiles. The black masking tape that's holding them in place is starting to come unstuck so that if somebody opens the door they start to dance in the breeze. National champion. Olympic Games. Professional debut. World champion. I watch them but they never fall off.

We stand around the sides because if we stand anywhere else, we'll be in someone's way. It's probably the biggest room I've ever been in, like a giant cave, but there isn't an inch to move. My dad talks to all the other dads while I watch Ned and Mushy, follow them with my eyes around the hall as they move from the skipping rope to the mirror to the punchbag to the pads. It's a funny place. The other dads stand there smoking their cigarettes, using the end of one to light another, and they all make jokes that I don't understand. There's always someone laughing. Someone cursing. Sometimes it sounds like they're angry when they're shouting at each other but they're not, they're only messing. A few of the dads stand out – they come in with big bags on their shoulders and everyone knows them because they always have nice coats or music tapes or videos in the bag and people want to buy them.

Ned and Mushy go to Repton two or three times a week but I'm only allowed to go once, on a Sunday, because I'm only seven. A man called Mick teaches me and the other children to keep our hands up so nobody can hit us, to keep our feet moving so nobody can catch us.

The older I get, the more I understand about Repton, and about how so many of the people who come through its doors have a past that they'd rather forget about, and maybe a future that they don't even realise yet. When people talk about Reggie Kray, I know who he is now; how Tony Burns, the head coach in Repton, is friends with one half of the East End's most notorious gangster twins; how Reggie and his twin brother Ronnie used to come to the gym sometimes and train. Ned is one of Tony's stars so one day, when Tony is going to prison to visit Reggie, Ned goes too.

Once you meet Tony, you never forget him. He's been in Repton forever, because he knows that for most young kids, like Ned, like Mushy, like me, the East End is one door after another being slammed in their faces until there's only two options left: go make trouble, or learn to box. Tony expects you to be on time, to train hard, to respect the green vest when you put it on. To win.

That's the Repton way. That's in my head all day as I get ready for my first-ever fight, carrying the weight of a hardened world title contender on my eleven-year-old shoulders. I'm in maths class. Maybe it's geography. Or history. I don't know, I don't care, although I'd welcome the distraction if only I could focus for long enough. The only sums I'm worried about are the ones that will be on the referee's card later tonight, whether the number of punches I've landed is greater than, less than, or equal to my opponent. Geography wouldn't even come into my mind other than finding out where in the country this other lad is from, if his club can match up against a Repton fighter. History? Look in the books and you'll see that Mushy won his first fight. So did Ned. I can't lose tonight. They'll both be at the fight. All of my family will be there. I can't disappoint them.

And when we pull up outside the working men's club in God knows what part of London and the man at the door says boxers to my left please, it hits me. We're not in Repton anymore. It's all so unfamiliar. I don't know where the dressing room is, or the toilets. I don't know what's down this corridor to the left any more than I know what's down the one to the right that the man is guiding me away from. An emergency exit, maybe, an escape.

I find the dressing room, hoping that I'll see a familiar face, someone that I can put my gear bag down beside, but I don't know any of these people. Maybe I'm in the wrong room. Everyone in here looks like they've fought a hundred times before. It doesn't take much for a young mind to get carried away, and I'm a body language expert now. The lad lacing up the black boots in the corner. He looks tough. The other guy with his foot up on the bench, stretching out his calf muscles while he talks to his friend. Tough. That lad chewing the chewing gum. If that's what he does to stuff inside his mouth, imagine what he does to lads in the ring.

I keep to myself, taking it all in without saying too much. They all sound a little different. Look a little bigger. They must be from the same club. Most of them are chatting like they know each other. My ears are pricked.

'Who are you fighting?'

'Dunno, somebody called A. Lee?'

I try to look without looking. I don't need to identify myself as the A. Lee in question right at this very moment. I see the guy, sitting on the bench in the corner, not a crease in his vest or a smudge on his shorts. But he looks like he's around the same age, so that's a win. The same size too, I think to myself, until I spot his bent knees, looming out over the edge of the bench into the middle of the room. I'm in trouble here.

When we get to the ring and touch gloves, I size him up properly. A good head taller than me, as expected. But I don't have time to do any more thinking and as soon as the fight starts, thirty seconds, forty seconds, those first couple of exchanges, I realise that he's not hitting hard and he doesn't have a plan. He's not that good. I'm probably not that good either, but all that matters is that I'm better than him tonight. Somewhere out there in the half-light, my mam and my dad look on, the rest of the family too.

When the first round ends, I go back to the corner and throw up.

As a kid, I never wanted to be a world champion. I just didn't want to let anybody down.

< >

We all live in a yellow caravan, a yellow caravan, a yellow caravan ...

I've always been the outsider; at least, it's always felt that way.

The Irish gypsy in England.

The English cousin in Ireland.

The white boy in Detroit.

We all live in a yellow caravan, a yellow caravan, a yellow caravan ...

I hear you. I hear you singing it, and we're sitting in French class trying to learn the difference between *Je suis* and *J'ai*. I hear you, and I know it's meant for me because it couldn't be meant for anyone else. None of the rest of you live in caravans.

You think you're smart because you know this about me. You think you have some sort of power over me. I thought you'd have a bit more sense. The only reason you even know I'm a gypsy is because your brothers box in Repton too, and they've told you. Are you thick or something? Do you not understand that if that's how they know me, that means I'm a boxer too?

I hate it here. This is prison we're in, not school, and if you show any sort of weakness, you better be prepared for others to pounce. There's grown men in here, full beards, and if they come for me, I'll have no choice except to fight back, so if it's all the same, I'd rather not draw their attention on me in the first place. That's why I don't go around mouthing off about being a gypsy. I know better than that.

And it's easy for me to hide. The black kids, the Indian kids, the Pakistani kids, they can't hide it. Even if they're English born and bred, they still end up on the wrong side when the battle lines are drawn.

I hear the rest of the class laughing now. You have your little victory. I feel myself getting angry. Angry to the point of tears. You'll be sorry you started this, I'm warning you:

'Wait till I get you outside.'

A lot of people don't realise I'm a gypsy. There's a perception that gypsies walk a certain way and talk a certain way and act a certain way, and I don't fit that mould, so unless people know that about me, they would never presume it. Adam Booth was my coach for a couple of months before he ever found out.

'Adam, imagine what you could do with a fighter like Tyson Fury?'

Tyson's a second cousin; our grandmothers are sisters. Everybody knows he's a gypsy – he calls himself the Gypsy King – but not everybody knows that we're related. Adam and I are chatting about a few other fighters while we work out in the gym and Tyson's name comes up.

'Imagine what you could do with that sort of style and that sort of ability?'

'Ah, I'll never train a gypsy.'

I keep shadow boxing in the ring, pacing my way through each step of my routine, and Adam's looking at me, wondering why I've started laughing.

'Adam, you know I'm a gypsy?'

'What?'

'I'm a gypsy. You're training one now.'

We've become good friends as well as coach and fighter,

and Adam's embarrassed. He starts tripping over himself to apologise – he didn't know and that wasn't what he meant, trying to put some context on it by way of explanation.

'Adam, stop. Just tell me, why did you say that?'

Because people don't realise I'm a gypsy, they say things around me that they would never otherwise say. Nothing hugely sinister, but it doesn't have to be. Gyppos. Knackers. Tinkers. The sideways glance. The tone of voice. It all accumulates over the years, a death by a thousand cuts.

I learn the difference between gypsy and Traveller at a young age. Subtle, especially for a child, but important. It's all about heritage. My dad shows me the photo of my two great-grandfathers in their Romany wagons, the newsprint of the paper yellowed from the years, and tells me the story of how they came to Ireland to escape the war and how, in this new country, a child from each side got married, deepening the bond between two families, ensuring that it would remain forever unbroken. Those two children were my dad's parents, my grandparents.

Being a gypsy is not something you think about. It's not something you choose. It's just the way life is.

It's only as you get older that you realise there's a special closeness to gypsy life. Between families. Within families. Family is everything, and summers are glorious. My dad's brother lives in Lewisham, on the other side of the river, and his sister is in Luton. Five or six caravans head off in convoy. Family, friends, dogs, chickens. All in. No man, woman, child, or beast left behind. Head west to Wiltshire, to Swindon, or maybe up towards Oxford. Canterbury. Eastbourne, by the sea, the beach, the waves that sweep you off your feet for a moment of panic and then release you unharmed to float in the glassy calm. And wait. Queuing up for ice-cream with our cousins. Those summers when we'd load everything onto the boat and head for Limerick, to my mam's side of the family. The introductions were always the same:

'This is my cousin Andy. He's from England …'

But I didn't feel English. They used to say in Bow that the only things Ireland ever wins are boxing matches and the Eurovision. I always wanted the Irish song to win. I wanted Steve Collins to beat Chris Eubank, and then I wanted him to do it all over again. I was Irish long before we moved to live there. London was where we lived, but Limerick was home.

We go to school, but before we do, we take the carpets and the rugs and help to stack them in the van so that my mam can do her deliveries, driving from site to site to sell what she can. At the weekends, we go down to the market with her and we try to help. Not getting in the way would be help enough. Or we go off with my dad, knocking on doors, dropping leaflets in letterboxes, calling into shops and offices. Five years old, six years old, holding on to the stack of paper with both hands, for dear life. Learn when you're young and you'll have your trade forever.

My dad's trade is as a tree surgeon, a landscape gardener. He works all over London, doing big jobs, doing small jobs. Some days he goes to people's houses to chop or cut or whatever it is they need doing. The days I go to work with my dad, I watch him. He never tells the man or woman that he's a gypsy. I know not to say it. You don't say it. You have to hide it.

It's just the way life is. Us and them, and we're the 'them'. The police are here again. You'd like to tell them not to bother taking out their little notebook and pencil, that they're only wasting their time, but that could be construed as cheeky, so it's best to say nothing. As usual.

We all know the routine anyway, we've known it since we were old enough to be allowed out of our parents' sight. When the police arrive, it's in everyone's best interests that they leave again just as quickly and, if possible, with even less information than they had in the first place.

One of the policemen produces a photo while the other wanders off to have a nose around. You take a look for a few seconds, long enough for it to seem like you're actually engaged in this pantomime, but not for so long that he might think you're being cheeky. Then he says his lines, and you say your lines:

'Does this man live here?'

'No, I don't know him.'

'Do you know his name?'

'No, I don't know him.'

'Have you ever seen him before?'

'No, I don't know him.'

Bow Triangle was a regular enough stop on their beat and a place of interest in their investigations, with good reason. There was always a trick or a deal or a bargain on the go, and a child might not realise it, but most of those little enterprises crossed the line. They were crimes.

It sucks you in. A lot of people that I grew up with ended up doing time in prison as they got older. If we had stayed in London, in Bow, immersed in gypsy life, I might have ended up in there with them.

When you're looked down on in a certain way, when you're pushed to the fringes of society and not accepted and there's no way in, it creates a lot of anger. I see it. All you can do is lash out, fight back, rebel. Young gypsy boys of nineteen or twenty go to the pub, arrive at the front door, and they're not allowed in. Or go to the bar, and they're not getting served. It's embarrassing. You don't want to let us in? OK, we're going to break your windows. The police get involved, or the papers pick up on it, and it feeds into the cycle, deepens it as it starts all over again. And the next time it's the pub down the road. No, we're not letting these fellas in because they smashed the other place up the last time. That's how the anger expresses itself, but you can't justify or excuse that kind of behaviour.

Back in the gym, I'm still shadow-boxing, and Adam is still stumbling over what to say. He tells me a story about one of the most naturally gifted boxers he had ever trained, a young gypsy who won every English title possible at underage level, but as he got older and turned professional, he didn't have the attitude to really kick on and make the most of his ability.

'I had too much trouble with the gypsies I did train before. They just don't have the discipline.'

Adam's right in a way, but there's a little bit more to it than that. Boxing starts as a way of discipline, a first commitment, an introduction to responsibility in life, as well as a social outlet. My mam and my dad were happy when they knew we were down in Repton – they'd drive us there themselves – because they knew that if we were there, we weren't getting into trouble or worse. And at that age, gypsy kids have a raw toughness, the kind that you can't teach, the kind that can only be chiselled out through growing up in a place like Bow site where showing any sort of weakness would be the biggest mistake of all. Gypsy kids, or Travellers in Ireland, are sharper, meaner, more mature at that stage in life. They're more physical and they can overpower kids from settled backgrounds; their strength and power trumps everything else.

But as everyone gets older, eighteen, nineteen, twenty, and the settled kids themselves mature in time, it balances out. Now the settled kids are more skilled because they've learned the hard way. They've had to learn to box because they couldn't rely on power alone and now, when they develop and the power levels are more evenly balanced, they win. The gypsy kids, the Travellers, get disillusioned. Even if they wanted to carry on, their culture, their society, is demanding their full participation. Get your trade. Go to work. Get married. Provide for your family. Be a man.

Over the years I learned that control, the discipline, the restraint that's befitting of a champion, but today I'm gone past that point. It's lunchtime and I'm ready for you. I find Pa, the only other gypsy in the school. He's my best friend growing up, close enough that he's like a fourth brother; a year older than me, a boxer, and the friend that I do everything with. I tell him what happened. I don't need to say another word because he knows what is going to happen next. He waits. We wait.

Pa sees you first.

'There he is now.'

I don't care who is watching. I don't care if you think it was only a joke. Nobody is going to treat me like that, to belittle me and my family like that, to make me the butt of the joke, to try to make feel small because of who I am. Sing your 'Yellow Caravan' song now. Go on. I dare you. Your words have consequences, and you'll know that soon enough when the punches start to land and you're wishing for me to stop this. I will. I will when I'm done. When you've learned.

And when we go inside and the headmaster turns to you first, the most obviously injured party, for your side of the story, I'll sit and I'll listen.

'What happened?'

'He beat me up, sir. He's a boxer. Look at what he did to me.'

Look at what I did to you? There's no denying that, nor will there be every time you walk through those school gates or sit back down in that French class for the next couple of weeks. The rage has ebbed, but I've no regrets, only a complete disregard for whatever punishment is coming my way. This office is meant to be a symbol of authority, it commands the obedience that is necessary to stop this place from descending into total anarchy a dozen times a day or more, but I'm not the least bit bothered about the scales of justice and how far they're tipped against me. Whatever price I have to pay now, so be it.

He's heard your side of the story. Now he turns to me.

'What happened?'

'He called me a gypsy and he kept on saying it and saying it and making fun of me in class and I told him when I get him outside I'm going to kill him and I did and that's it, so you can do what you want.'

I don't know if the headmaster's impressed, or sympathetic, or already completely jaded and just wants to quickly close the book on his latest problem of the morning. He pushes back his chair and motions for us to leave.

'Right, go on, go back to class.'

The drive takes us fifteen minutes. My dad drops me and Roger to the door of St Francis Boxing Club.

'Go on in, see if your cousin is inside.'

We go in, but it's nothing like Repton at all. Limerick is nothing like London.

We don't live in the city. We're building our new house in a place called Daly's Cross, in a little village called Castleconnell. Out on its own in a two-acre field in the middle of nowhere. It wasn't a surprise when my mam and my dad told us that they'd had enough of Bow, that we were going to move home to Ireland permanently in 1998. They had been planning it for a while. I love Limerick, love it when we come here on holidays, but I don't want to live here. My life, my friends, they're all in London. Now I have to start all over again from scratch.

That's the point. I'll come to thank them for it in time. It changes the course of my life.

But right now, I'm thirteen and I'm miserable. Lonely. I don't know where to go or what to do, and even if I did, I'd have nobody to do it with.

I get up in the morning and go off to work with my dad on whatever job he's on. Saturdays, we go into Limerick with my mam to the markets and then afterwards I hang around the city with Roger for a few hours, in and out of shops, until we spend whatever little bit of money we have on a video game that will do us for the week, hour after hour, every night. Or down to Frank Lee's, the petrol station just down the road from the house, and flick through their library of videos until we find one that we want to rent. One of the imported Asian ones. We watch them all, and most of the ones in Xtra-vision in Castletroy too.

But there are only so many video games and films in the world.

Work is work. Cutting back bushes and tarmacking drives is only glamorous when school is the other alternative. Otherwise, it's hard, it's tiring, it's pretty monotonous, and it's what I've been plaguing my mam and my dad to let me do for years.

'When am I giving up school? I want to go to work. Let me go to work. What am I doing? I'm like a fool, everyone is making fun of me for being in school. None of my friends go anymore. They're all out working. Why do I have to keep going to school?'

And every year the answer would be the same.

'You're not giving up. We'll talk about this next year.'

And then next year comes and by August you're trying to find your jumper and wondering if you'll need any new books or if the old ones, wherever they are, will do for another year. Now that we're in a new country, it's easier to let me have my way.

The thing is, I was actually good at school, even though I always had one eye on getting through it and getting out of there as quickly as possible. I was in the top three when we did the London Reading Test, the standardised test you take when you leave primary school – not the top three in the class or in the school: the top three in all of Tower Hamlets, which is a big borough. I started secondary school in one of the best classes, but I wasn't interested. And when they moved me into a lower class – the stupid class, the trouble-makers' class – I was even less interested.

I'd be in my seat by nine o'clock to sign the first register of the day, but once that class was done, I'd find Pa and the two of us would be off up the road. We'd go to the park, or to the chip shop, and go out the back to where they had the pool table or the arcade machine. We'd be back in school in time for the midday register, gone again, and then back one last time to sign the register at four o'clock before heading home.

I need boxing more than ever now that we're in Limerick. I might never get to speak to another teenager again otherwise. Not that I do much chatting when I'm up in the club. My dad drops us in to Mungret Street three nights a week, we go in, train hard, say our goodbyes, and get a lift back home. It's not a place where you go to make friends.

It doesn't take me long to realise that I'm fighting at a level above everyone else in St Francis. That's the Repton effect. I won my first seven fights as an amateur in London, but in my eighth I lost to a kid called Aaron Gardiner. I'll never forget his name. Pa warned me about him. He lost to Gardiner a year earlier, and he wanted me to level things up on his behalf.

'You've got to beat this guy. You've got to beat this guy.'

Pa didn't bother coming to the fight that night, which was just as well, but I still had to go back and explain myself to him afterwards.

'What happened, what happened? Did you beat him? Did you get him?'

'No, he beat me as well.'

It wasn't the last time I came up against Aaron Gardiner. The gods of the draw looked kindly on me in the schoolboy championships the following year. I got my own back. A stoppage.

I kept improving, kept winning, and I started to see myself as a boxer. It became part of who I am, the thing that made me distinctive, the thing I told people about myself. When I won my first schoolboy titles in England, other people started to see me as a boxer too. My teacher came up to me in school with a copy of the *East End Advertiser*, our local paper, and congratulated me. I played it down, told him that it wasn't a big deal, and there was a part of me that believed that too. I expected to win. But when they read out my name at assembly, my chest puffed out a little bit nonetheless.

By winning a couple of schoolboy titles, I far surpassed anyone's expectations of me. Of the six kids in our family – Dawn, Mushy, Ned, me, Roger and Hayley – Roger was always the one earmarked to be the boxing star, even more so than Ned.

Repton laid the foundations, put all the building blocks in place for me but because Roger is a couple of years younger, he still needed a bit more time there to develop, and when we moved to Limerick to different coaches with a different way of doing things, a lot of what he had learned was undone.

Roger was too proud to say no, even when the demands being made of him were crazy. He came to me one day.

'Andy, they want me to fight tonight.'

'Tonight? Against who?'

'Dunno. They want me to go down to Dungarvan. They're stuck and they need me to fight.'

'What did you say to them?'

'I told them I'd do it. I'm getting ready to go now.'

I would never take a fight on that short notice unless I had been training hard and, more importantly, unless I was certain that I wasn't being sold a pup. But when Roger got down to Dungarvan, he was fighting against Amir Khan, who was a world medallist at that stage and already showing all of the talent that would win him his Olympic silver medal. Roger was thrown in, with no preparation, on a couple of hours' notice, just so Khan could have his fight. Roger lost that night. He was still a teenager when he gave up boxing a few years later, but he always had a huge role in my corner throughout my career.

I come to love St Francis. The coaches there – Kenneth Moore, Finbarr O'Brien and Shane Daly – spot my talent straight away. They have me in against the best in Limerick, then the best in Munster, and see that none of these other lads can really trouble me. A week or two after I first go to the club, Shane organises a big sparring day on a Saturday with lots of boxers from different clubs coming to St Francis. I keep warm and loose as Shane calls all of the other boxers in, pair by pair, but he never calls my name. I wait around for hours, watching everybody else take their turn, before I ask him about it.

'Am I sparring or what? I've been here all day. What's going on?'

'There's nobody here for you to spar. There's only one fella here and he's a junior. We can't put you in with him.'

'I came down here to spar. I'll fight this lad. Put me in.'

This guy is a few years older than me and an Irish champion, but that doesn't matter. When I get into the ring I'm well able for him. Shane can't believe the level I'm at. He needs to test me out for himself.

'Will you do another couple of rounds with me?'

I get right back in there to go again, and I'm well able to keep up with Shane as well. He might not have known too much about me before today, but he knows me now.

When I move up to national level, I become the first boxer from the club to win the Irish youth title since Ken Moore's dad Seamus won it thirty-five or so years earlier. I start getting called into national teams. I'm still working with my dad, doing whatever jobs I have to and pulling my weight, but boxing is my number one priority. When we meet up for camps, I realise that I'm not the best in the country. Roy Sheahan is. But that only makes me even more determined. You can't judge much from a bag session in training, but the running sessions are a clear marker of who is leading the way, and I always make sure that I'm up there with Roy.

I never wanted to be an astronaut or a pilot. They'd ask those questions in school, and whatever you'd say, you'd never really believe it. Gypsy boys go to work, pass their driving tests as early as they can, get a van, start doing their own work, meet a girl, get married young, get a trailer, settle down, travel around. That's the set path, and it's a good life, and one that's very hard to break out of.

But the more time I spend in Irish squads, or when I meet coaches like Billy Walsh and Zaur Antia and want to impress them, the more I realise that my life doesn't need to be that way. When I left school and gave up on my education, I closed a lot of doors and found myself in a position where I had nowhere else to go. I don't have options. I just have this and now I have to follow it through to the end, even if it turns out to be a fool's errand.

I want to succeed so that I can be somebody. Boxing is the only shot I have.

⟨ ⟩

I know every inch of the Bog Road in Castleconnell and every inch of its gravel knows the soles of my runners: it's rubbed them away over hours and days, one step at a time, and now it's just foot and ground with barely a pretence of rubber left to separate them. If you need me, you'll find me here, alone. You wouldn't fit two cars side by side here, but then again, you'd rarely need to. I own the Bog Road. Two miles out. Two miles back. A thousand times.

My hood is up and I splash through the puddles. On a dry day, I could run through the fields, through the bog itself, a token gesture to take the edge off the punishment. I'm running so much that my legs ache. Shin splints? Growing pains? Who knows?

I don't want to be here in the rain. I'm tired and I'm sore, from training and from work. I don't want to be here at all. I was still finding distractions as morning turned to afternoon, the little hand of the clock judging me from the wall. Excuses. Putting it off and putting it off. I felt sore before I even pulled on my running gear, anticipating the pain that was to come. Before I took that first step out the door, I'd have paid five hundred euro not to be here now.

Nobody knows I'm here and if I wasn't, nobody would care. We were told exactly how many sessions to do, the specifics of what was expected in each one. Military detail. Next time we meet up, the coaches ask how much we all got done. A trust exercise. Everyone says that they've done it all but you know who is lying. Why would you lie? Who are you cheating, only yourself?

You have to do it. Look at my T-shirt: it says it right there. Just Do It. I put the aches and the rain out of my mind for just long enough so that I'll get up, and I go. The negativity evaporates. I run and I stare into the fields and I think of the ring and of my next fight. What I'll do when I win. What I'll say. What everybody else will say about me.

Sometimes, for a second, my mind will drift years down the road.

And the new middleweight champion of the world …

But then it's back to here and now.

You get it done. You always do. You push yourself. You go through the pain, and when you come out of it on the other side, you feel better than you ever have before. Training is the journey, and you need the journey. It's the journey that gives you confidence when everything else starts to waver. Knowing that you've given every inch, every day. No corners cut. No stone unturned. Knowing that you're out there working when nobody else will. That you've dedicated yourself, given yourself over wholly and completely. Allowed yourself to be totally consumed.

Knowing that you're ready.

I've the phone in my hand before the second ring has even finished. The rest of the family have never seen me move so quickly, a masterclass in reflexes and reaction.

'I'll get it. It's Emanuel Steward ringing to talk to me'. I call back over my shoulder to nobody in particular but if they heard me, if they understand me, not a budge. Nobody peeks their head around the kitchen door after me to see if I've completely lost my mind or why I'm getting so excited about a phone call.

A phone call? It's Emanuel Steward, the most famous boxing trainer in the world. Who else could there be: Angelo Dundee made champions of Muhammad Ali and Sugar Ray Leonard, two of the all-time greats; Lou Duva had Pernell Whitaker, Evander Holyfield and more; Cus D'Amato trained Floyd Patterson, found Tyson. But Emanuel Steward doesn't just have one fighter or a few. He has the Kronk Gym. He built a factory of world champions in Detroit. The man behind Tommy 'The Hitman' Hearns twenty years ago, and he won world titles at five different weights. The man behind Lennox Lewis and Naseem Hamed more recently. These guys know. When world champions go to war, with their belts and their everything on the line, they want Emanuel Steward in their corner. They want Emanuel Steward to have their backs.

And he's ringing Daly's Cross, Castleconnell, County Limerick, to talk to me. The dishes are still soaking in the sink beside me as I pick up the phone. It's Christmas Day 2002.

I know it's Emanuel Steward because I've been expecting the call. Not for long – an hour, maybe two, nowhere near long enough to process what's actually happening. The last time the phone rang, it was someone looking for me as well.

'Andy, Damian McCann is my name …'

I don't know Damian, have never met him. He introduces himself, explains that he is the secretary of Belfast Amateur Boxing Club. Tony Dunlop, one of my coaches with the Irish national squad, is his cousin and Tony is sitting beside him now, on Christmas Day, waiting for Damian to get to the point.

'I've just been on the phone with Emanuel Steward, the boxing trainer, and we were talking about you. I hope you don't mind but I gave him your phone number. He's going to call you later.'

We chat for a minute and I thank Damian and hang up the phone, the excitement still hanging there. This doesn't make sense, and of all the possible explanations – even if you consider the phone ringing again to belong somewhere on that list, Emanuel Steward waiting patiently on the other end for me to get up off the couch and answer it – I know in my gut that the most plausible outcome is far less glamorous: the phone won't ring again for the rest of the evening. Emanuel Steward won't call the following day either, or the day after that, and I'll spend the rest of the Christmas holidays waiting, those hours filled with thoughts of what it might be like to be a professional boxer, and wonder about if I could make it and how far I could go. And just as I become consumed with the possibilities, eventually the phone will ring again, but it won't be Emanuel. It will be Damian or Tony, understanding and apologetic, as upset as I am that Emanuel had never called but offering a solution, that out of our shared disappointment can come an opportunity. The dream doesn't have to be dead. I can still turn pro, but here at home, with Tony as my trainer. Here it is, the first broken promise of my professional career. All of those horror stories that I've heard, of young talents promised the world and then used and abused, that's what will happen to me. Professional boxers end up broke and professional boxers end up broken. It's a world of sharks and snake-oil salesmen, most of them barely disguised, and nothing about it is to be trusted. It's part and parcel of being in amateur boxing; it defines itself as much by what it isn't as by what it is, and it isn't the seedy sweatshop of professionalism. It wears that skepticism and disdain for the pro game as a badge of honour.

But I'm worrying over nothing because the phone does ring again later that evening, just as Damian said it would, and from thousands of miles away, Emanuel's voice sounds familiar, like we've spoken many times before and now we're just picking up where we had left off the last time. And all of that doubt and uncertainty disappears because now we're on the phone and I know what it means for a man like this to be calling me.

He speaks and I listen. I press the phone harder into my ear with my left hand, as if it might somehow bring me closer to Detroit or I might hear Emanuel better. My right hand jabs. Jab. Jab. Shadow boxing in the kitchen, my footwork and motion limited only by the length of the extension cord.

'Andy, you beat Gonzales …'

Emanuel wants to talk about the World Junior Championships in Cuba earlier that year. Jesus Gonzales wasn't even on my radar. Ismail Sillakh: that was the name that had been lodged in my head in the run up to the tournament, since the row about the gloves. A training camp against the English team, everyone trying to squeeze out that final per cent or two of fight sharpness before flying out to Santiago. They've brought their best middleweights, two guys, Tony Jeffries – future Olympic medallist-in-waiting – and another lad, Joe Smyth. They're here to test me. I know it. No other reason. Get a good read on me before the tournament, see if I'm someone that they need to keep tabs on. But this thing about the gloves, I don't understand what all the fuss is about. Loads of other fighters have already sparred in there today, and there's been no chat about glove size, but Terry Edwards, the English coach, is getting very animated all of a sudden.

'What gloves do you want to wear? What gloves do you want to wear?'

Another Tony, Tony Davitt, is there as my coach. I'm looking at him, and he's looking back at me, and neither of us really have a clue what the English play is here. If they have me wondering what they're at, that's probably good enough for them. They've distracted me a little bit, introduced that tiny sliver of doubt. I honestly couldn't care less what gloves we wear, and neither could Tony.

'I'll let you guys decide, Terry. Me and Andy are happy with whatever.'

'The big gloves so, the sixteen ounces, not the fourteens.'

Fine. Whatever. Let's spar. Joe Smyth gets in with me first. Bang. His nose is pumping blood. Definitely broken. A complete freak accident too. I didn't even hit him hard. It was just a jab straight down the middle and whatever way it landed, it bust him wide open, the drops collecting on the canvas in a small cherry-red pool.

'Jesus Christ, what are you doing? Joe, come here, come here.'

The English are furious. Whether I meant it or not is completely immaterial to them. There's no way Smyth's nose will have healed in time for him to box in Santiago. You cocky little so-and-so. We'll put you in your place.

'Tony, are you ready to go? Get in there now.'

I don't know if anyone's even watching us.

'Get us a fresh towel there. Has anyone got any ice? Keep your head forward, Joe.'

Jeffries is already warmed up, waiting, while everyone else fusses over Smyth. Bang. He's on his arse too – not knocked out but caught cleanly enough that he had no chance of staying up. That's it, get him out of there, we're done sparring against you lot. Terry Edwards is back in my face again.

'Oh yeah, you did well in there but there's a Ukrainian in your division, Sillakh. You won't beat him.'

You won't beat him. You won't beat him. You won't beat him. The words echo in my mind like a challenge. Now I have to beat him. When we get to Santiago, the walls drip with sweat and humidity, and every time I go to breathe, I wonder if my lungs will ever taste fresh air again or if it will just be the same stale heat from now until the day I die. Marco Periban is still picking himself up and putting himself back together, and I'm being slapped on the back like I've just won the whole tournament. Like that's the job done.

Two wins, two stoppages, against the Slovakian and now against Periban, the Mexican. You've done us proud. To even get into the quarter-finals and give yourself a shot at a medal is more than anyone could have expected. Nobody could beat Sillakh. Sure he won the gold medal at the cadets in Azerbaijan last year, the best under-seventeen boxer in the world. A year on, a year bigger, a year better. There'll be no no shame in losing to him. Nobody can take what you've done away from you now anyway.

I go to the bathroom before I get my hands wrapped. Someone's in my stall. 'My' stall. I'm not superstitious but I've used the same stall for the last two fights and I'm not changing anything about my preparation. Not now. I'll just wait. I go back in to hit the pads, try to find that sweet spot between getting loose and heading to the ring already dripping in my own sweat. They're right. I've done well. I won't disgrace myself in here. I'll give this lad a right test, but when I lose, I can be happy.

The hall is packed, the heat of a thousand bodies smothering the ring. Find someone who loves you the way the Cubans love boxing. There's not even so much as a fan there to offer some relief, never mind air conditioning.

I see Sillakh. He's carrying himself in that effortless way that champions do, a million miles from the arrogance of the pretender. If you could start from scratch and build a boxer, you'd build Sillakh: tall – at least as tall as me, if not taller; muscles that would make you think twice before stepping into his range; intimidatingly angular features. There's no point even trying to get a read on him. Within those sharp edges, his face is blank, completely emotionless. An ice-cold killer. I'm pretty sure he's not even breathing.

And as I step up onto the apron, my mind clears and all of the talk of the last few days, the negativity recast as achievement, evaporates.

I'm winning this fight.

I step into a fog, and my mind makes its subconscious choice. In this draining heat, I've enough energy to either box or to remember, but not to do both. Everything is blank now. I feel it when he hits me – it hurts – but I make sure that I hit him back, that I leave more than a little reminder on him. That I hurt him too. Two big light-middleweights. Punches landing cleanly. I know that I'm still in the fight in the final round because I hear Tony's voice and I register it; it slowly filters into my sleep as though he's calling my name over and over again to try to wake me.

'One down, Andy. Let them go, let them go. Yes. You're level. Let them go.'

And when I wake, I see Sillakh again. I look him in the eye, and I know he has nothing left, his gloves like lead as he tries to raise them into a guard, panic written all over that emotionless face. I step in.

One, two. One, two. One, two.

'Andy, you beat Gonzales …'

I was never supposed to beat Gonzales. An Irish boy? I was never even supposed to get that far.

Emanuel was meant to be there the night that we fought. He was the national director of coaching for the US amateur boxing programme, and Gonzales was his golden boy. Jesus Gonzales of Phoenix, Arizona. The US national champion. But when Emanuel went to fly in a few days earlier, Havana airport was closed. Hurricane season in Cuba.

'… *You should come over here to Detroit now and come train with us in the Kronk Gym.*'

I don't have the energy to fight Gonzales. I don't even have the energy to warm up. Don't panic, I tell myself, just think. If you can't rely on your arms and your legs, rely on your brain. You know how Gonzales is going to fight. A southpaw, like you, fighting behind that right-hand jab. He's short. You're smart. Box him, and don't get dragged into a scrap. Box him, and he won't be able to reach you. Keep your distance. He'll have to commit. Let him do the work. Let him come to you. Then you'll have him where you want him.

In theory, it's foolproof; in practice, less so. I can't move my legs. It's barely forty-eight hours since I fought Sillakh and they're still finding bits of me in this ring, so it's no wonder I can't bob and weave my way out of trouble, making Gonzales miss. He has no problem finding his range, but when he comes in close to throw his punch, he leaves himself open. Just enough opportunities for me, exhausted, jaded, to beat him.

'I'll get you a deal and we'll turn you pro.'

The day of the final, I'm a dead man walking. Fighting in Cuba, against a Cuban, Noelvis Veitia. We're in the dressing room and Tony has a bottle of water in his hand, using it to spray my face. I'm sure he's talking to me, but I can't hear him. I sit in my chair, an outsider looking in on my own reality. He's taking off my gloves, not putting them on. He must not be happy with something. Now he's unwrapping my hands. Maybe there's something wrong with the tape. He sprays me again.

I'm on the bus in my tracksuit when I start to snap out of it. Garrett Dunne is in the seat beside me, my roommate for the last few weeks.

'Here, Garrett, what happened?'

'You lost.'

'I lost the final? What happened?'

'Ah, he was better, he beat you.'

'What? I mean, did I do the … did I get my medal?'

'Yeah, you got your medal. There, look.'

Garrett reaches across until I look down and see the silver medal hanging around my neck for the first time. That's nice.

'Did I get up on the podium?'

'Yeah, you were on the podium. Do you not remember this?'

Garrett's confusion turns to laughter as he realises that I genuinely haven't a clue what he's talking about. The fight, the dressing room, the medal ceremony, it's all a giant blur of nothingness. Completely empty, both mind and body. In the middle of the night, I wake for long enough to realise that my face is on fire. The next morning, when I look at myself in the mirror, I'm covered in cold sores all around my nose and across my mouth. I see the medal on the table, where I must have left it. You gave it everything, I think. I fall back asleep again.

'Come to the Kronk. You'll be a world champion within thirty-six months.'

Two days after we fly home, I'm back in Limerick, in a stranger's garden painting their windowsill. A car drives by, and someone spots me. Go on, Andy, good man yourself, we were cheering for you. I give the back of the car a thumbs up as it disappears off down the road, and then go back to my paintbrush. Tomorrow, it'll be the lawnmower in someone else's garden. Nothing's changed, and yet everything has, because it's Christmas Day and I'm standing in my kitchen on the phone to Emanuel Steward.

'Well, Andy, what do you think?'

I think any eighteen-year-old in their right mind should say thank you very much, put down the phone, start packing their bags, and kiss their mam goodbye. But winning silver at the World Juniors has planted the seed of a dream and, right now, my green Irish singlet is the most important thing in the world to me, even more important than the red and gold shorts of a Kronk champion. I can't hand it back. Not now. Not with the 2004 Olympics on the horizon.

I thank Emanuel, and I try to explain.

'I will come over there, I'd love to, but I'm going to try to go to the Olympics in Athens. I hope we can talk after that, but I want to see if I can go to the Olympics.'

Emanuel must be a little bit taken aback by my response and by how definitive I am, but if he is, he doesn't let it show.

'Alright, that's good, Andy. I understand that. We'll keep in touch. Maybe you can come over to visit us some time before the Olympics for a few days. But if not, you'll definitely come over afterwards. I'll be watching you in the Olympics.'

〈 〉

There's order and control in the final moments before a fight, in the quiet calm of the dressing room, before you make that short walk into the arena. I take a moment to myself and I pray.

There's a line in the song 'High' by the Lighthouse Family that has always stuck with me: 'Even the impossible is easy when we got each other.' It's a pretty cheesy song, and an unusual place to find a prayer, but that's exactly what it has become for me. I clear my head of all other thoughts, I sit in silence, and I think about those words.

Even the impossible is easy when we got each other.

I pray every night, and I draw strength from it. When I talk to God, I talk to myself. I talk honestly. I confront the fears and the anxieties that I wouldn't be brave enough to say out loud. I zero in on my positive thoughts, the affirmations, and I repeat them until I accept them as part of me. My faith is my psychology. It gives me strength.

There are times when injuries threaten to ruin all of my best-laid plans, when I solve one problem and it is replaced just as quickly by another. When the road I'm on seems too long, too impossible, when the doubt and fear and worry descend like they will never go away. I work hard and I train hard, and I never stop believing in myself because I believe in God.

Faith is deeply personal. Organised religion and spirituality is not for everyone. At times, it isn't for me. I drift away from it and find a new way of thinking, of understanding the world and myself, but I'm eventually drawn back. I find answers there, and great solace.

In my late teens and early twenties, there's no wavering; my faith is a constant, reassuring presence in my life. I discover it for myself in my own way. My family is not really a religious one, but my mam is. We go to mass together sometimes, and when I stop going as a teenager, I find that I miss it. I drive down to the village in Castleconnell by myself every Sunday morning at 9.30am. When I'm away travelling with the Irish team, Zaur and I try to find the local church in whatever country we're in and go to mass together. When I'm in Detroit, I find a Catholic church down the street on Grand River. I walk there at first, and later Emanuel's wife Marie starts coming with me. She picks me up, we drive to mass, and we spend those few hours together on a Sunday.

I never pray to win – except one time. I know it's much more important that I pray that God will look after me in the ring. Worrying about winning is exhausting. It's counter-productive. I find peace and freedom in believing that if what I'm doing is right, if it is in God's plan for me, then I have nothing to worry about.

‹ ›

I'm alone in my room, trying to concentrate on my book, but my eyes and my brain are just going through the motions, leaving the words sitting there unread on the page. I might as well be in Athenry as Athens; no matter where you are, the world largely looks the same when you're lying on your bed waiting. Every so often, I go out to the kitchen and ice my hand, which is done out of necessity, but it's nice to have the distraction as well.

I check the clock again. Some time around now, in between the teams from Iran and Equatorial Guinea, my Irish teammates will be walking out behind the tricolour into a packed Olympic Stadium for the opening ceremony. Nobody would be more proud than me but, in the circumstances, it's a risk I'm not willing to take.

There's only hours to go. Tomorrow is the first day of boxing and I've my opening fight against Alfredo Angulo, the Mexican. The biggest fight of my career. I remind myself that I'm not in Athens to walk in a parade, even if it is a once-in-a-lifetime opportunity. I'm here to box, and to win, and standing around for hours on end in a suit sounds like a terrible way to prepare. I need to rest, I need a proper night's sleep, and I need to make sure that my hand is OK.

My hand. It hasn't been right for months. The last two years of my life run through my head on a loop. The sacrifice, the struggle, every ounce of effort that I put in to make it here. And for what? I go to get more ice. The worry hangs like an albatross.

The first day I meet Gary Keegan, he shakes my hand, congratulates me on my perfofmance in Santiago, and invites me to be one of the best amateur boxers in the world. He tells me his vision. High Performance, he calls it. No more exceptions. No more excuses. No more scrambling for silver linings of mediocrity in performances that are all cloud. When he stretches out a long strip of red electrical tape on the ground, and challenges us to step across it, to trust him, to join him on a journey towards being world class, I'm ready.

Everything changes. No more drinking on trips. The dogmatic insistence on doing things a certain way – our way – goes out the window. Our way hasn't been working. Gary brings in a powerlifting coach. A nutritionist. A performance psychologist. The best in the country. But High Performance isn't just a revamped training plan or better support or a new set of rules. It's a lifestyle, an attitude, a way of seeing yourself. International tournaments don't have to be hard luck stories, fighting against the odds, with any hint of success celebrated as an overachievement. When we step in against the Russians, the Cubans, whoever, we need to remind ourselves that we're full-time elite athletes, that nobody is working harder than us, and that we have the best of the best behind us. We need to feed off the confidence that it brings.

Gary is the director of boxing's High Performance Unit, and he brings in two coaches to work alongside him: Billy Walsh, and a little middle-aged Georgian man with barely a word of English but the best boxing brain I've ever seen. I idolise Zaur Antia. I've always seen myself as a boxer in that traditional European–Russian mould, but I've had to teach myself: studying good fighters in camps or on tape, emulating them, trying to mix their style with my own. I might be doing the same things that they are – I might even be doing them better – but I'm reaching in the dark. Zaur teaches me how to follow a sidestep hook, why one punch will work when another one won't, why to look for an uppercut to the body. He teaches me the technique and he teaches me the logic. That understanding, that's what frees me to believe in myself.

I win my first senior national title in 2003, then my second a few months after my nineteenth birthday. It turns a few heads, but I brush it off with the arrogance of a naive teenager; I think it will always be this way. But there's no doubt that boxing is where I belong. When everything else is stripped away, I still have that. The Olympics sits there, the greatest show on earth, my beacon, my north star. To qualify, to be an Olympian, to win an Olympic medal: that's an achievement that will change how people see me.

But now I'm here and I'm miserable. Lonely, more than anything. In my room or in the canteen thumbing the pages of *Pound for Pound*, one of Sugar Ray Robinson's biographies, while everyone else breezes across the Olympic Village in groups of friends or teammates. I'm the only boxer on the Irish team. Nobody else qualified. I spend more time with Billy than with anyone else, but our technical sessions and other bits of training are done in short, sharp blocks, and they're long days otherwise. Sleep. Train. Eat. DVD. Train. Eat. Another DVD? Maybe. Sleep.

When I meet the other boxers in the Olympic Village or in the boxing hall, they're the same faces that would be at any multi-nations tournament or at Europeans. The draw is the same, the weigh-in is the same, the pre-fight routine is the same. I feel ridiculous, like I've wasted the last two years putting the whole Olympic experience on a pedestal and building it up to be something it's not. Michael Carruth once said that he had to go to his first Olympics in 1998 to experience it, in order to be able to come back and win gold in Barcelona four years later. Walking out of the tunnel into the Olympic Stadium for the closing ceremony a few weeks later, I'm blown away by the buzz. This is what I missed. It is special; I just never fully connected with it. Maybe it would have all been very different if I had gone to the opening ceremony that night instead of sitting in my room by myself.

I've a week off after I beat Angulo in the opening round. *El Perro*, they call him, The Dog, but I never let him off his leash. A week is a long time to be uneasy. I've been living with the same concerns since the start of the year, since I injured my left hand. The problems start while we're preparing for the European Championships in Pula, Croatia. We're taken up into the Wicklow Mountains for a team-building exercise but, by day four, I've had enough.

It starts out as great craic, bringing out the Bear Grylls in all of us. If we want food, we have to forage for it, or win it by doing tasks. We're sleeping in tents and out in the open in bivvy bags – those one-man sleeping bags that seal up into a little pod – but now I'm cold and I'm wet and I'm not one bit happy. My clothes are wet, my socks are wet, and for some reason we're still trudging through muck and mountains playing these stupid games. Every day, we keep telling ourselves that we are elite athletes, and we're expected to perform like them, but none of us have eaten properly in days. I can't sleep. Find me any other top country in the world that's preparing like this.

'What the hell are we doing here, Gary? What is this?'

The trip is nearly over and we're going home soon, but I have my little hissy fit anyway. I'm past the point of caring. Gary and the others leave me to simmer away on the bus back to the National Stadium, and when we arrive, we're told to get changed. Four days in the wild and now we're straight back in to training as usual. The minute I hit the bag, I know I'm hurt. It might be out of sheer frustration, or maybe my body is run down and a bit weaker after our little *Hunger Games* in the hills, but my left uppercut catches the bag awkwardly. Every time I clench to make a fist, the tendon flicks back and forth across the knuckle. Torn.

These European Championships double as the main Olympic qualifier and now, just as our main training camp is about to start, I can't throw a punch. Everyone else ramps up their preparations while I sit there and hope for the best. Gary suggests that I try some visualisation. Time's not on my side. I've nothing to lose. I trust him. I close my eyes and start at the beginning: open the front door of the gym and walk in, into the dressing room, get changed, hands wrapped, gloves on; I go out and warm up, shadow boxing, skipping, a few minutes on the bag; then I get into the ring and spar.

All the time I'm watching anyone around my weight who has been brought into the camp to spar. How they move their feet and their head, the type of punches that they favour, trying to decode their rhythm and their style. I make notes and then rebuild them in my mind until a fully-formed sparring partner stands right there in front of me, vibrant, welcoming my challenge. My body twitches, ever so slightly, as I throw a punch or slip one in return. It's working. When we fly out to Pula, my left hand has healed, and I feel fast and sharp. Even if the visualisation had no physical impact on me at all, even if it was all a placebo, I feel ready, free and confident.

Just as everything seems to be starting to click, it all unravels again just as quickly. I win my opening fight at the European Championships easily but back in the dressing room, when I take my right hand – my good hand – out of the glove, I know immediately that something doesn't feel right. I wind the wrapping off it, slowly, but my hand is stiff and I can't move my fingers properly. More than stiff, it's sore. I try to close my hand to make a fist and I can't. Broken, three stress fractures across the centre of it. I can't open or close doors, I can't even pick up a cup, so there's no way that I'm going to be able to glove up and throw a punch.

Even an eternal optimist would start to falter now. To have one injury was bad luck, but a second is an unusually cruel twist of fate. Two wins away from the Olympics, and if I withdraw, my best shot is gone, maybe never to come again. There's one final qualifier still to come later in the year, but I don't quite fancy pulling up a stool in the last-chance saloon with every other desperate fighter in Europe. I need to somehow find a way. I know it has to be now.

I bluff my way to a win against Darren Barker in the next round. Instead of boxing with my right hand, I use it as a mental weapon. I shape to throw it, show Barker that picture, and then feint and set up my left instead. I have to throw one or two punches, the jolts of pain shooting up into my shoulder an unnecessary reminder to be sparing, but I'm careful. I never let him see him I'm hurt. The morning of the quarter-final against Nikola Sjekloca, Gary takes me to see the doctor and we get my hand injected with an anaesthetic.

Winning that fight against Sjekloca, guaranteeing a European Championship bronze medal and securing qualification for the Olympics, should be a moment of pure elation. I feel nothing but relief, and that soon ebbs away. When we fly out to Bugeat in France for my final pre-Olympic training camp, I can't spar at all. Kenneth Egan offers to come out with us as my training partner, to keep me company, which I'm very grateful for. But when I get to Athens, the only companion I have is the one I don't want; my hand heals, but never fully.

When the middle Saturday of the Olympics comes, a lot of the team have competed and finished and I'm one of the last big Irish stories, two wins away from the country's first boxing medal in twelve years. I'm good at separating my fights from their significance, so that all of my concentration and energy is on the moment between the first bell and last, and not on the other distractions and consequences that surround it. There's a saying I love that I try to apply throughout my life in boxing: 'Matters of small concern should be treated seriously. Matters of great concern should be treated lightly.' It's from a Jim Jarmusch film, *Ghost Dog: The Way of the Samurai.* When I'm asked for an inspirational quote to paint on the wall of the National Stadium, that's the one I give them.

I like my dressing room light and breezy before a fight. No tension. Any deep thinking should be long done at this stage. I don't know why, but things are different today. I start to dive into my emotions, and bounce off them, using them as fuel, as motivation, when the only motivation I need is named Hassan N'Dam and will be standing in the ring in front of me. Concentration and focus and mental energy are not limitless resources. If you let your attention slip and divert it away from your performance and onto the context or the consequences, it's a mistake. There's already enough pressure on this fight. I don't need to address it, or to add to it myself.

I get to the boxing hall early. It's part of my routine, even though I've already boxed there. I want to look around, start to build a picture in my head of the sights and the sounds and the smells. Where the dressing room is. What the walk to the ring will be like. How long it will take. How close to the fans I'll be. How loud it might be come fight time. The fights are just starting – mine is one of the last in the evening session – but as I turn to go out into the arena, one of the officials stops me. I'm not allowed.

There's no point in arguing. I don't need the distraction. Down in the warm-up area, we start to get ready, but Billy and I hardly say a word to each other. I can't get out of my head, falling into every trap that I'm usually so good at avoiding: magnetising the fight, building it up, inviting more and more pressure on to myself. Billy is at a loss. He's never seen me like this but now is not the time to question it. He thinks that it's a deliberate choice, and if this is how I'm choosing to prepare, so be it.

A sharp knock on the door, the signal that it's time to go. I step through the curtain into the arena and the enormity of the occasion hits me. Totally unnerving. When I fought Angulo a week ago, there were only a handful of people in the crowd: my brother Roger, a friend of ours, Pat, and Finbarr O'Brien who is one of my old coaches from St Francis. Now, it feels like half of Ireland has descended on Athens with their tricolours and their *Olé Olés*. A lot of the team are here, and their families too. It's hard to make out faces in the stands, but I can't miss the six lads bouncing around in their giant leprechaun suits. I'm totally distracted by the atmosphere and before I know it, N'Dam is coming straight at me. The fight has already started.

All week we've been preparing for N'Dam to take the fight to me, like Angulo had, allowing me to box my natural fight and pick him off on the counter. We start to feel each other out, but he's never the one closing the distance. Every time I step in, he takes a step back. He's light on his feet, moving around, baiting me into impatience. A completely different fighter. He saw me coming, double-bluffed me, and now he's trying to beat me at my own game. I want to fight, and when he draws me in, he attacks quickly off his back foot in a burst and then gets back out of there before I can respond. His punches are scoring. Most of mine are not.

He's putting a puzzle in front of me, and I can't adapt or solve it. I'm totally out of control. I don't have a proper read on him or on the fight, and I'm losing. Technically, he's not a good fighter – he's not hitting me cleanly, his wild swings landing with his forearm more than with his glove – but physically he's imposing: raw, rough and with a lot of power.

After two rounds, I'm four points down, 16–12. Not the position I expected to be in, but still in the fight, and I'm grateful for that much. Billy doesn't panic when I go back to the corner between rounds, but he doesn't have his usual calming presence either. I can hear the urgency in his voice.

'You're down, you need to pull this back. Attack, attack. Be aggressive.'

He prays that I hear him, that the message gets through before this fight slips any further away from me. Maybe he can see that I'm out of sorts, that he needs to try to provoke some sort of reaction, but it only makes me more anxious. I pull two points back in the third round, but I still need a big performance to win the last round by three and get myself out of a mess that is entirely of my own making.

Time is against me, and N'Dam is no fool. We come together in the final seconds, both of us throwing as the bell goes. Billy looks at me as he's taking off my headgear in the corner.

'Did I do enough?'

'It's a countback.'

I win the last round by two points and the fight finishes in a draw, 27–27. Now the scores from all five of the judges are being quickly recalculated by the computer to split the two of us and decide the winner. Terry Edwards, the English coach, has been helping Billy, standing behind the judges to watch the scoring as it happened, and judging by the tone of Billy's voice, the vibe from Terry isn't good. It's not going to add up in my favour.

Hope is the only thing I have left, and I'm hanging onto it now as I meet N'Dam in the middle of the ring. We share a quick hug, respectful. He's still, studying the canvas, while I pace back and forward, sending out all of the outward signs of a confident victor on the off-chance that the perception can tip the balance in my favour at the eleventh hour. I bless myself, and then bless myself again. The stadium announcer's Greek means nothing to me, but N'Dam's hand is raised, mine still at my side. I drop to my knees and punch the canvas twice, hard, in frustration.

RTÉ are waiting at ringside so that I can explain to the country what went wrong, but I just want to get out of there. I don't want to be hanging around where people can see me and console me in that typical Irish way that we often do. Ah well, you lost, but you did well and you did us proud. I don't want to be a good loser; I just want to get out of there. I am crushed, devastated, disgusted.

I do the interviews as quickly as I can and then I'm taken into the doctor's room to have my hand checked as a precaution to make sure that there was no further damage done. Before I know it, I'm in the back of an ambulance being rushed away to an Athens hospital.

A Greek doctor shines his torch in my left eye, shakes his head, and scribbles a note before turning the torch on me again. There had been no new problems with my hand when the doctor checked me over post-fight, but before he signed off, he noticed that my pupil was huge, extremely dilated to the point where it was nearly only pupil. I had to go to hospital. He insisted.

Billy sits beside me in the back of the ambulance so that I have some company. My mam had flown out for the N'Dam fight, and she rushes out behind us as soon as she's allowed. Time becomes this abstract thing as we sit and wait and everything around us seems to slow to half-pace. I don't have much to say for myself and everybody else is worried into silence. The doctors put us at ease; the problem is nothing too severe or sinister, but they have to keep me in for observation until the specialist is back in work on Monday and can sign off on me. It's Saturday night, winding its way towards the early hours of Sunday morning.

My mam pulls her chair around and does her best to console me.

'I know it's hard but I hope you're proud. You were the only Irish boxer out there. Everyone doesn't make it this far.'

I spend two nights in hospital, where the cameras can't find me and nobody can ask their million questions. I have the time and space to think without being rushed into snap reactions and knee-jerk judgements. By the time I'm discharged, I'm starting to come to terms with everything. Talking to my mam really helps, and she's right: I was the only Irish boxer to qualify, I am still very young, I won a fight, and then I lost on a countback which couldn't have been any closer. This must be how it is meant to be.

And I swear that I'm done with the Olympics. For two years, I spent every day working towards it and every night worrying about it, and I'm done. I just have one final engagement to attend to when we get back to Dublin, the official team homecoming reception with President Mary McAleese in Áras an Uachtaráin.

That's where I meet Maud.

❬ ❭

I get up, go downstairs to pour myself a glass of water, and then go back to lying on my bed and resume staring at the same spot on the wall. The house is empty, everyone out at work, the normal rhythm of life as it should be. My suitcase sits in the corner where I left it, still waiting to be unpacked.

For the first time in two years, I'm free. There is no schedule with the where and when of every second of the day accounted for in painstaking detail. If I don't put in my miles on the Bog Road today, nobody will notice or care. I can do what I want. Eat what I want.

I feel trapped. Castleconnell, Limerick, ticks with the excruciating normality that is needed to get from one end of the day to the other. I have to get away.

I ring Adam Forsyth. I first met Adam in Bugeat in France when we were there for our final training camp before the Olympics. He was there as part of the Australian team and we got chatting a bit. The day I was released from hospital in Athens, I bumped into Adam again and one of his team-mates, Ged O'Mahony. We went for a drink, and one became a few.

I needed to blow off some steam. I hadn't touched a beer in months, since winning the senior title the previous December. I never said it to anyone. It was my little sacrifice, a statement of my seriousness. If I was going to be an Olympian, that was part of the deal. But once I was beaten, I cut loose. I started hanging out with Adam every night, criss-crossing Athens as we bounced from one Olympic party to the next, and then I'd crawl into bed at four or five in the morning, sleep until one or two the next afternoon, and shake off the fuzzy head and furry mouth to do it all again. It was the only way that I could completely detach, divorce myself from the Olympian that had been three years in the making and all for nothing.

Adam answers.

'Where are you? What are you up to?'

'I'm in Ibiza. I'm here with some friends. Come over!'

'I've a thing to do. I'll try to fly out to you tomorrow.'

I pack my bag and head for Dublin. The following day, after the presidential reception, I jump on a flight. It's dark when I land and Ibiza is already stirring to life. Adam and his friends are in Pacha, one of the famous dance clubs. No time to waste. I drop my bag at my hotel on the way and go straight to meet them.

It's €40 just to get in the door, €15 for a drink at the bar. No special treatment for Olympians here. Not that it deters us. The two of us are putting them away as quickly as the barman can get them out to us. A couple of women come over to say hello, and then a bit of a crowd starts to form. If we're buying, they're drinking. *Uno más, por favor* – with a wave of the hand in the air, the accepted gesture for a round in any language. We're laughing, joking, leaning in closer so that we can be heard over the thumping bass line. Too close for the liking of some of the local lads, apparently. I've no idea what they're saying but the general gist of it is pretty unmistakable.

I don't even see the bouncer or have time to politely enquire how I'm the one in the wrong. I probably am. He drags me out of there and turfs me out the door into the dawn light while his mate follows, Adam in tow. It's morning, or will be soon. The back of the club is like a building site. Scaffolding and other bits and pieces. Adam is furious. Before I can stop him, he takes a hold of the scaffolding and puts all of his heavyweight strength into it until it comes crashing down around us.

'Ah, man, you shouldn't have done that.'

Now it's definitely time for us to leave. We start to walk away – left or right, it's all the same when you don't have a clue where you are. The back door of the club clicks behind us.

'Adam, run. RUN.'

Five or six security guards come charging at us. I run but Adam stands his ground. He wants this fight. He's well able for it. But no amount of rounds in the gym will prepare you for a six-on-one. It's like whack-a-mole, except these moles have telescopic batons and they know how to use them. I get a smack across the side of the head for my troubles as I go back to grab Adam and pull him away. We take off at a sprint.

'We shoot. We shoot. Stop. Stop!'

I didn't see any guns but it's not really the moment to be calling their bluff. I go one way; Adam goes another. I've no idea where I'm going but I keep running and I don't look back. I look down and realise I've only got one shoe. Keep running. I find myself back in the town and stop to sit down. Blood coming out my ear, and my foot is cut to bits. I've nowhere to go, no idea where my hotel is. I sit and wait for the police to come and find me. Eventually they do.

'Come on, take me. Is my friend OK?'

'Your friend is in hospital.'

It sounds like he's in trouble. They don't even need to help me into the back of the car. I'm happy to go. The clock on the dashboard says 7am. At the hospital, we wait and we wait. When Adam comes out, he's wearing nothing except for his hospital gown and a massive bandage on his head. It could have been worse. The police take us down to the station and lock us in a holding cell.

'What happens now?'

There's no phonecall home allowed. They leave us sitting there all day, and all we can do is laugh at the stupidity that has put us here in the first place. It's hours before a lawyer comes down to meet with us. The local fixer for idiot tourists who need to be bailed out. Within a couple of minutes, the cell door opens and we're free to go.

We each give the lawyer €60 for his trouble.

'You've to go to court on Tuesday. My advice, get on your plane.'

We don't need to be told twice.

‹ ›

I spot her across the room – out of the corner of my eye, I'm sure, because that's how it happens in the movies – but it's not long before I'm turning my head to make sure she's still there. Eoin Rheinisch, the canoeist, is telling me a story. We haven't seen each other properly in a while, but I'm totally distracted. When I look, I catch her eye. Is she looking over at me, or is she looking and wondering why I keep looking at her?

I try to place her but I can't. I don't think I've ever seen her before. I'd know her if she was an Olympian, and I don't think she's involved in one of the backroom teams. But there are a lot of unfamiliar faces floating around Áras an Uachtaráin. Hers just happens to be the one that has me captivated.

I wasn't really looking forward to this. The formal occasions are never really my thing. A bit stuffy. The pin-striped blazer and beige chinos. It's the kind of thing that can go on all night but I've already got my excuses ready. I'm staying in Kenneth Egan's house in Clondalkin tonight and I've to go and meet him. It will give me a reason to slip away.

But it's good to see everyone again if nothing else. Nice to dip back into the bubble for a minute. A nice reminder that we've all been through this together. I meet the President, and she congratulates me. Outside, there's a photo on the steps.

Back inside, I see Billy and we go to catch up. She's there again, chatting in a group that I don't know that well.

'Billy, who's that over there? The blonde girl over by the door, do you know her?'

He's not taking me seriously. Billy mentions something offhand about sailors, and goes straight back to whatever point he was making. When we've finished chatting, I say my goodbyes and quickly slip away to get a taxi.

My phone rings in my pocket. Billy again. There must have been something else that I was meant to stay for.

'Hey, Billy, I've just jumped in a taxi. Is everything OK?'

'Yeah, everything's grand, Andy. I'm here with this young lady. Would you like to speak to her?'

'What? Yeah, put her on the phone, put her on the phone.'

I couldn't have been gone more than a few minutes and Billy was up to his tricks. When I left, he went over to the group, introduced himself, and started making small talk. Mid-conversation, Billy pulled his phone out of his pocket to call me and then, unannounced, tried to hand it over to this young lady:

'And, sorry, your name is …'

'Maud.'

I wait, but Maud never takes the phone from Billy. He tells me that he'll call me back later, and when he does, he has her number for me. When he hung up the phone, he asked if he could have her number to pass on to me, that I'd like to call her myself. I head off out with Kenneth for the evening, back around to his local in Clondalkin, but there might as well be three in our round now. I'm texting away in between snippets of chat in the pub. I tell Maud that I'm flying out to Ibiza in the morning for a few days. I don't even get the chance to suggest meeting up when I get back. It's Wednesday evening; she leaves on Sunday to go to Paris for a year to study.

But my trip to Ibiza is short-lived and by Saturday afternoon, I'm back in Kenneth's garden, barbecue heating up and beer in hand. We kept texting back and forth while I was away – without most of the detail – but now that I'm back, a free man, maybe there's a chance we can meet up before she leaves. Not going to happen. Maud is at Electric Picnic, a one-day festival that they're running for the first time in the grounds of an old country estate in Laois.

I've tried. We promise to keep in touch, and who knows, maybe we'll bump into each other again some other time. I go back to my burger, and after a few more beers, when talk of taking the night into town is inevitably floated, I'm fully on board. It falls to me and another one of the Irish boxers, Alan Reynolds, to keep the party going. It must be after 3am by the time I finally take myself off to bed. My phone rings as I'm lying there. It's Maud.

'Hey, I'm at a party in Temple Bar. Do you want to come over and meet me?'

'Sounds good, yeah, I'll see you soon. Send me the address.'

I'm up out of bed, dressed, and back into a taxi like lightning. I look like a man who has been out for the day. I look like a man who has just gotten out of bed, I'm sure. I'm doing whatever I can to fix myself up in the back of the taxi when the phone rings a minute later. Maud again, except this time, it's a different voice on the other end.

'Hey, Andy, it's Maud. Sorry, that wasn't me that you were just speaking to. My friend had my phone. I don't think you should come over.'

Maud explains, mortified. She is at a party in Temple Bar but she left her phone down for a second when she went out of the room. Her friend Aisling had picked it up and thought it would be a good idea to pretend to be Maud and ring this guy Andy that she had been talking about.

'Oh, OK. Well, it's too late, I'm already on my way.'

When I get there, Maud comes down to meet me. There are too many people upstairs. Too loud. It's after four in the morning. Saturday night spills out into the streets around us. Taxis. Takeaways. We walk through the staggering chaos like ghosts, oblivious. We've nowhere to go but we walk. We walk and we talk.

Maud's beautiful. She's funny. I know nothing about her but I want to know it all.

She tells me the story of how she ended up in Áras an Uachtaráin. Her first cousin, Maria Coleman, is a sailor, and Athens was her second Olympics. Maria travelled up from West Cork for the presidential reception, and she was allowed to bring a guest so invited Maud to go with her. Maud had already made plans to go for dinner with friends, a last chance to say goodbye before she left for Paris, but changed them so that she could go to the homecoming instead. 'You never know,' Luke, her brother, told her, 'you might meet the man of your dreams.' Luke got the eye-roll he deserved.

We walk for hours, the last of the stragglers long gone home to give us peace, for a second, until morning comes and a new city stirs back to life. We say goodbye, not knowing when we'll see each other again, and Maud leaves for Paris that afternoon.

I call her every day. I call her to hear about her new apartment, the course, her classmates, the city. The phone bill arrives: €1,300. It would be cheaper to go to Paris. So I do. I fly out to visit for a weekend. She brings me to the café she likes. She introduces me to her new friends. Falling hard and falling fast, we both know that if we were living in the same city, we would surely be together.

Maud gets sick, suddenly. She reassures me, but they fly her home from Paris and bring her straight into hospital in Dublin, so I'm right to be concerned. They keep her in for weeks while they treat her. My alarm goes early in the morning, and I get into the car and drive from Limerick to Dublin to be with her. I visit her every day, spend all day sitting by the side of her bed. It's just the two of us and nobody else while the doctors and nurses buzz around us, checking charts, pagers beeping. We get to know each other. She tells me about her love of music, art, languages. She's in a band. I meet her parents, her brother and her sister. I drive home to Limerick at night and come back up again the next morning.

I know we're from different worlds, that this isn't how it works. I know that bright, brilliant, educated young women from South County Dublin who have the world at their feet don't end up with a gypsy boxer from Limerick via London who left school at thirteen. She must know it too, but she doesn't care. I tell her everything honestly, about my life, my heritage, my family, anything that she would want to know. Nothing shocks her. She tells me that she doesn't care about what I am or what I've done. She accepts me for me, and it makes me fall even more in love with her.

She plans our first proper date. A concert. Of sorts. She has two tickets to the National Concert Hall, a recital by Maxim Vengerov. He's a violinist, she explains, and not just any violinist, one of the best in the world. I might think I know a little bit about culture because I'm not obsessed with cars and clothes and money like a lot of gypsy boys, because I read books and rent a few films with subtitles, but this is a whole new league.

We arrive at the National Concert Hall; all the men are dressed in tuxedos, dickie bows, the women in beautiful gowns. I wear what I always wear: a hoody, tracksuit bottoms and trainers. I don't belong here.

But the performance starts and I'm completely blown away, transfixed by this man on stage, the way that he's communicating with the violin, the energy he brings to the performance. It's not dull or boring. It's incredible. There's something very special about music which has existed for hundreds of years on a piece of paper, brought to life to exist in a moment, and then it's gone again.

He receives standing ovation after standing ovation. My hand is still bandaged up, so I can't even clap to properly show my appreciation. Maud asks if I enjoyed it, and gets her answer with a cheeky grin that betrays my fascination.

'He's not bad that fella, is he?'

She invites me in to be a part of that world, full of colour and art and creativity. We go to the theatre, but I don't quite get it at first. I don't know how to believe in it, how I'm supposed to see anything other than people standing on a stage pretending to be someone they're not. I fall asleep during a few plays at the start. I don't really know how to say it to Maud, that I'm not really sure that this kind of thing is for me. She doesn't go out of her way to force it on me either. Her dad buys us tickets for a play, *The Bull*, and it's like nothing I've ever seen before in my life. It's based on the old story of the *Táin Bó Cúailnge*, but it's more than just a straightforward script with actors and dialogue. It's a powerful, immersive experience that really draws me in, and there's a lightbulb moment where I suddenly understand where the art is in all of this. And I love it.

Every time we go out, we seem to meet somebody that Maud knows. I keep getting introduced to new people, her friends – male, female, friends that she's known since she was four or five, friends she went to school with, friends from college. I don't have any of that. Pa was my only friend and we lost touch when I left London and drifted away from that life. I see how close Maud is with some of her male friends, and I think they're taking liberties. A kiss on the cheek. A hug that lingers a little too long. I get jealous, angry. My gypsy roots have shaped me, left me with their rigid, conservative view of the world, but that imprint changes and evolves with time. I find my own place in life, a place that won't bind me to any narrow-minded traditionalism.

In the beginning, when I introduce Maud to someone I know, to a gypsy, I worry. I've always worried about what people think of me, and now I'm worried about what people will think of her. If they'll know she's not a gypsy. Gypsies don't marry outside the community, don't even openly have relationships with non-gypsies. Gorgeys, we call them. If they do, they're disowned, cut off entirely by their friends and families. I shouldn't care but, when we start going out at first, I do.

Just as I have to learn how to live in Maud's world, she has to learn how to live in mine. She loves hearing stories about my family, learning about our history, our culture. When Christmas comes, we've been going out for a few months, and I decide that it's time to bring her home to meet my parents. I tell my dad.

'I'm bringing a girl back, Dad. I'm going out with a girl from Dublin. Her name's Maud.'

I have to tell him. He'll find out anyway.

'She's a gorgey girl, Dad. I want to bring her back here for Christmas to meet you and my mam.'

I know what he'll say, so it doesn't come as any surprise.

'You won't bring any girl into this house.'

'Wait until you see her, Dad. Wait until you meet her.'

'Oh, so that's why you've been up there all the time? Well, she won't be coming into this house.'

I understand where he's coming from. Maybe if I was in his position, I'd react in the same way too. But it doesn't change how I feel about Maud, and I know once he meets her, he'll see things differently.

I bring her down anyway, the day after St Stephen's Day, to meet the whole family. My dad comes in for a minute to say hello, and then goes back into the living room to sit down again. I know he's listening in to the conversation as Maud chats to my mam and my sister Dawn in the kitchen, trying to see for himself what she's like. By the end of the visit, he's sitting down with her on the couch, going through the family photo album, answering all of Maud's questions. It doesn't take long for her to win him over. He can't help but like her.

< >

Tommy Hearns studies the sandwiches on the plate in front of him, rigorously, as if picking a punch, before finally settling and making his choice. Teaspoons politely clink in cups, a fire roars, and Emanuel Steward is sitting beside me. Two years have passed since that first phone call and here we are now, finally meeting for the first time.

It was a long time before I was able to explain the sequence of events that brought me and Roger to the front room of Damian McCann's house in North Belfast that day in October 2004. A long time before I fully understood them myself. When I hung up the phone that first night, Christmas Day 2002, everyone was still sitting in the living room, their lives utterly uninterrupted.

'Who was that, Andy?'

'Emanuel Steward just rang me, Emanuel Steward.'

My mam could see my excitement even if she didn't fully understand it.

'Who's that?'

'The American trainer Emanuel Steward. Do you not know him?'

I tried to explain, to give a crash course in the legend, give this giant of a man his due place in boxing history and, at the same time, make sense of the fact that he had just been on the phone. To take what sounded like the fiction of an overactive imagination and get across the fact that, no, this had really happened, like Alex Ferguson phoning up a young footballer, or Francis Ford Coppola picking up an actor off the street and casting him in *The Godfather*. Not to play Michael, but maybe in time.

It all started with Damian, and he told me the story. A boxing fan first and foremost, he had written to Emanuel in the summer of 2002, Lennox Lewis's world title defence against Mike Tyson, surely expecting the letter to be shuffled from one unopened pile to another unopened pile before it was read months later by someone in Emanuel's office with a generic thank-you letter maybe dropped in the post to acknowledge it. Either that, or else forgotten about forever. So when Emanuel not only read it, but also phoned to thank Damian personally and to speak with him, he was as surprised as anyone.

Most people would be happy to leave it at that, a personal phone call, but Emanuel knew who he was now, and Damian was determined to keep that connection alive and turn it into a relationship. A few weeks before Christmas he put together a parcel to send to Detroit: an Ulster Rugby coat, some local newspaper clippings about his club, Belfast ABC – most of which Damian had written himself – and a few about me and my silver at the World Juniors.

The package arrived on Christmas Eve, and when Emanuel phoned again on Christmas Day, he wanted to know about the tall, skinny white kid who had beaten Gonzales in Cuba. That was the kid he was interested in. That was his future world champion.

Now he's here, with Tommy Hearns, to officially open Emanuel Steward's Belfast Kronk Gym in the back of the old Duncairn Presbyterian church off the Antrim Road as you head out of the city. It's still same building that used to be the home of Belfast ABC, the same people, but you wouldn't recognise it now. They've spent hundreds of thousands of pounds over the years to renovate it and now it has been transformed again with red and gold livery. Emanuel and Tommy are in the thick of it all, making time for every autograph and photo.

Later that evening, when the crowds and the BBC have gone home, we go for dinner. Emanuel sits at one end of the table beside me, Roger, and Tony Dunlop and we eat and talk for what seems like forever. Emanuel talks about superstars from a different world, fighters who only exist in the papers and on TV, as if they were his closest friends. Knows more about them than some of them know about themselves, it seems. Every name comes with its own story, and over the years, I hear so many of them so often that it's impossible to distinguish when and where I heard them first.

He tells me the story of how he moved from Bottom Creek, West Virginia, to Detroit with his mother as a young boy and how as a teenager he became the best bantamweight in the city, then in the country, and put that abstract claim beyond dispute when he won the most prestigious amateur tournament of all, the national Golden Gloves, at eighteen. He could have turned professional, but the promoters were all pimps and the fighters were all hoes. His family needed money and support, not empty promises and broken dreams, so he became an electrician, working on the lines for Detroit Edison. He drifted away from the sport but his boxing brain – that natural understanding of fights and fighters – never dimmed, and when his younger brother James started boxing a few years later, Emanuel could see every flaw in how he was being trained. He knew there was a better way but there was no point in tinkering around the edges; it was all or nothing. He took over James's training, and when James won the Detroit Golden Gloves, Emanuel was asked to stick around and coach the city team for that year's national tournament. Like any good raconteur, he knows how to deliver the punchline: that year, 1971, his Detroit squad won more national titles than any other team in the country.

I listen, totally captivated, to his tales of those first days in the Kronk, a city-funded community hall no different from any other in the world, training whatever local kids showed up to the sessions he'd put on when he was finished in work. There was nobody for them to fight in Detroit, so when the weekend came, they piled into his station wagon and he would drive across the Midwest to Illinois, Ohio, wherever they could find fights. He would drive there and back in the same night if he had to, marathon trips while his young protégés slept in the back. When they got to an age where it was time for them to turn professional, Emanuel was determined that their talent wasn't going to be squandered by the same cowboys he had tried so hard to avoid himself.

There's a photo on the wall in his house, from a newspaper clipping, of Emanuel and three young boys – thirteen, eleven, and nine, at a guess. Two of the three went on to be professional world champions, and the other was an Olympic gold medallist. When he tells me about those kids he started out with in the Kronk, I know he's talking about Tommy Hearns, Milton McCrory, and Milton's little brother Stevie.

That was only the beginning of it. Mike McCallum's name is mentioned in passing. An observation about Evander Holyfield. An anecdote about Lennox Lewis or Oscar De La

Hoya. Years later I'll be listening to the same stories about the same characters and, in an instant, the sheer depth of Emanuel's boxing life will hit me afresh, and everything will start to feel that little bit surreal again.

He tells me enough stories to fill books and libraries, but that night at dinner, he keeps steering the conversation back to me. My plans. My future. He's insistent, leaving little room for discussion or for me to counter.

'You're coming to America, Andy. You'll come live with me in Detroit, and I'll train you in the Kronk.'

He's not worried about the fact that I lost at the Olympics, they're just computers, he reassures us. He sets expectations at the highest possible level, and it's not bluster. Those eyes see hundreds, if not thousands, of prospects every year. They knew when they looked at Jesus Gonzales that they were looking at a star in the making, so any man who outclassed him like I had done must be worthy of consideration. I had done it with the odds stacked against me, he tells me. A fighter like Gonzales, coming up through the American amateur system, was training with top-level fighters every day. I was in a much smaller country, with much fewer resources. Imagine what I could do if I moved to America.

'You'll be a world champion, thirty-six months. You'll see.'

It feels like Emanuel has made up his mind on me, and now he's transformed from trainer into salesman. This is his pitch. I know that. But this man has no more mountains left to climb in boxing and he's showing this sort of interest, this energy and excitement, in me. It's hard to see the small print. Of all the European fighters he has trained – he'll go through the list again if he has to – he has never taken any of them from their professional debut through to a world title. That's the challenge that he has set for himself now, and whether he's ultimately proved right or wrong, he's certain that he has found the next fighter that he wants to take his shot with.

He draws me into his world, just to give me a taste, a glimpse at my own future. A couple of weeks later I'm ringside at the Mandalay Bay in Vegas, waiting to hear 'Enter Sandman' and see Vitali Klitschko come down the ramp and stop Danny Williams.

Vegas is exhausting. Depressing, really. The lights, the noise, every step bringing a new needy demand for your attention. Never mind your attention, your money will do. As we're checking into our hotel, there are hundreds, thousands of people gambling away money they know they can't afford to lose: unthinking robots, the process of taking a coin from their cup, dropping it into the slot, pulling the arm, and staring blankly at the screen now fully automated and lacking in any sort of emotion or enjoyment.

We're so busy, thankfully, that the slots and roulette wheels and poker tables are all background noise. In and around the Mandalay is Disneyland for a young boxing fan, the guest list a couple of pages ripped straight from the hall of fame honour roll. De La Hoya. Cotto. Hopkins. I get pictures taken with all of them, and by the time I get back to St Francis a few days later, I already have them all developed to show off.

It was a trip in three parts. Our first stop before Vegas was in Chicago where I met Perry Mandera and his business partners. Emanuel introduced Perry as he would an old friend, a Chicago businessman and philanthropist who had made his millions by starting his own transportation company. Trucks and logistics were his day-to-day, but boxing was his one true love, and a cent spent on the sport was rarely a cent wasted in his eyes.

Emanuel wanted them to back me financially. He had already put his initial offer on the table – a $50,000 signing bonus for me to turn professional, and a small allowance of a couple of thousand dollars a month to cover my living expenses. It wasn't a life-changing amount but it was a genuine and reasonable offer, and if it was up to me, I probably would have taken it. I didn't know how to negotiate, and I didn't have anyone that I could turn to to negotiate for me. I didn't have a manager or an agent or an advisor, but Damian had put me into this position to a large extent, and now he felt a responsibility towards me to make sure that I was properly looked after. Politely but firmly, he turned Emanuel down.

'You've got to understand what Andy means to Irish sport. They want to keep him amateur so that he can go to the Olympics again in Beijing. There's all sorts of funding and sponsorship opportunities on the table. I'll have to convince him to give all that up to turn pro, and I won't be able to do it for that kind of money.'

Damian put a peg in the ground: a $250,000 signing bonus plus the allowance. Emanuel didn't balk.

'Leave it with me, Damian. I'll call you soon.'

Emanuel always had a plan. Back in the early nineties, Perry and a few others had tried to get in on the ground floor with a heavyweight named Danell Nicholson, who turned pro after just missing out on a medal at the Barcelona Olympics. Emanuel trained Nicholson, but the financial support came from this group of investors. Nicholson got to a good level, but never really made it, and after he retired in 2003, Perry was ready to get a group together again and back another fighter. Perfect timing. Emanuel was insistent that it should be me.

I flew into Chicago with Tony Dunlop on our way to Vegas, and Emanuel and the investors met us there. I couldn't get a read on them. They had never seen me box, so how did they know what they were getting. I said all the right things, but I only spoke when I was spoken to, happy to let Emanuel do the talking on all of our behalves. He stuck to the same messages he had been repeating to me all along: once I turned pro, I would be a world champion within thirty-six months. Now, did they want in, or not?

We left them to think about it as we flew out to Vegas, and on the way back, we made our third and final stop. Detroit.

⟨ ⟩

W e slow down outside an old building, non-descript in every sense except for its redbrick finish and the chipped, once-red rail that winds its way across the front. It looks like a library or a school, has that air of bland, functional bureaucracy, but the car slows to a stop to let us out. This must be it.

5555 McGraw Avenue is unremarkable and yet somehow impressive. Much bigger than I expected, for one thing, two storeys tall and the same width as three or four houses. I anticipate the sounds before we even step through the door. A rope skipping off the floor like a metronome. The leather of glove on the leather of the bag. The urgent instructions dispatched from the periphery of the sparring ring. Instead, Emanuel opens the door onto a group of local kids locked in the unique sense of battle that a game of pickup basketball brings. This isn't a boxing gym.

Emanuel beckons us and we follow him down the stairs into the basement. At the other end of the long, narrow corridor is a door with its unavoidable challenge hand-painted on the front.

THIS DOOR HAS LED MANY TO PAIN AND FAME.

He opens the door and a blast of heat, desperate to escape, hits us. We follow him into the small room and immediately we are in the heart of the Kronk Gym, as suffocating in its intimacy as in its temperature, with nowhere to hide. No wonder the place produces so many champions. The intensity of focus is deafening. Barely a head turns as Emanuel walks in. The fact that a twenty-year-old white kid has followed in behind him, sticking out like a sore thumb in a room full of black fighters, hasn't even registered.

He goes into a side room, and leaves me and Tony for a few minutes to take it all in. It doesn't take much imagination to drift back twenty or thirty years and see Hearns or Kenty or the McCrory brothers in that ring. It might be that long since the walls were painted, and with the exception of a few minor upgrades around the place, not much else has changed.

The pipes above our heads let out a low hiss as fighters pair off and rotate in and out of the sparring ring, the centrepiece of this one-room operation, set low to the ground in the middle of the floor. Others skip or shadow box or punch the bag, oblivious, but every other eye in the room is on the ring, dozens more of the greats watching down from the pictures as they wilt on the wall. Three men, maybe four, too old to be fighters, sit on wooden benches underneath, their commentary loud enough only to be heard by themselves.

Painted high on the wall are the messages that I would come to read several times a day, every day, over the next seven years of my life.

TURN UP THE HEAT.

WHEN THE GOING GETS TOUGH, THE TOUGH GET GOING.

NO PAIN, NO GAIN.

HARD WORK PAYS OFF.

THE BIGGER THE REWARD, THE BIGGER THE SACRIFICE.

Emanuel returns. 'How would you feel about getting in there for a few rounds?'

I'm only here for a look, not to get thrown into a sparring session with someone who is looking to chew the new kid up and spit him back out just as quickly. I've no gear with me. But they're only excuses, and I've already seen enough to know that excuses don't fly in this room.

'Now? Sure, let's go.'

He shouts over to a fighter on the other side of the room, roughly the same shape and size as me but a few years older.

'Hey, Ronald, can this kid borrow your boots for a few minutes?'

Ronald is Ronald Hearns, son of Tommy and a fighter already starting to collect names on his own pro record. I pull on his boots and his headgear and wash out my gum-shield. Emanuel tosses me a pair of gloves. I start to loosen out, get my feet moving, throw a few punches, and I feel everything around me stop: no more skipping rope, no more punchbag. Silence, except for Emanuel's shout. 'Hey, K9. You're up.'

At this, a huge man standing at the side of the ring, dressed in civvies, lets out a roar. 'Oooooh, fresh meat, fresh meat, here we go, here we go.'

If the rest of the gym hadn't already stopped, we've their undivided attention now. Emanuel might have hoped that I'd feel at home but, as a short, stocky fighter bounces through the ropes and into the ring that is clearly his domain, there's no doubt in my mind that I'm behind enemy lines. Cornelius Bundrage, 'K9' to his team-mates and friends, a man with the swagger that you might expect from the most dangerous fighter in the Kronk Gym. This is nothing out of the ordinary for him; young kids who think they can fight come through that gym door and go out again just as quickly, rethinking their place in the boxing world after just a few rounds up against him. This is as routine as a Monday afternoon comes:

he's an undefeated twenty-win pro on his way to the top, a light middleweight with a vicious edge, and if Emanuel asks, he has no problem putting manners on me like he has done to so many wannabes before.

He's not hanging around either. He comes straight for me, ready to put me on my back there and then. I switch into autopilot and get my feet moving. It will buy me a few seconds to figure him out, if nothing else. He tags me once or twice, but I'm leaving a little bit on him too, and outside the ring, the volume is turned up again.

'Woooo, come on, K9. Get that white boy. That's it, get that white boy.'

The bell goes. I go back to my corner, expecting Emanuel or maybe Tony, but Tommy Hearns is leaning over the ropes instead. He's enjoying this – everyone is, by the sounds of things. He gives me a few tips, a few punches he has spotted that might give Bundrage something to think about, and sends me back in.

I'm not used to fighting three-minute rounds, and I can hardly breathe in the heat, the sweat already running off my forehead and into my eyes. I focus on Tommy's instructions, and I catch Bundrage a few times. He's muttering away to himself, and I can sense that this isn't how these initiation sessions usually go. The hostile edge hasn't put me off; I am relishing it, and changing it.

'He's good, he's good. This white boy can box, K9. Don't let him whoop you.'

We spar three rounds, maybe four, before Emanuel signals that that's enough. It is. There are no referees, no scorecards, but we have a room full of judges and it's clear who has won their decision. People who hadn't even noticed me come in half an hour earlier are coming over to fist bump, touch my glove, and find out how the hell I had ended up in the Kronk in the first place.

You can fight, boy, you can fight, one guy tells me. The adrenaline is still surging. In any gym, there's no commodity more valuable than respect. I know that I have earned that much at least.

Someone once told me that whenever you experience déjà vu, it means that you're following the path in life that is meant for you. As everyone else goes back about their business, and Emanuel pulls on the pads to do a bit of work with me, I get the strangest feeling that I have been here before.

‹ ›

I pick up the phone and dial Damian's number. I'm straight with him. The last thing I want is to talk myself out of the decision I have already made.

'I'm not going to Detroit. I'm going to stay amateur and go to the Olympics again.'

I'm being asked to take a huge leap of faith into the unknown, and as I stand at the edge, peering over, I can't bring myself to jump.

The money is there. Emanuel makes sure that Perry and his partners in Chicago get word of how I'd handled myself in K9's doghouse. They push their chips into the middle of the table. A $250,000 signing bonus, more money than I or anyone I know has ever seen in their lives. Everything is in place, except for my signature.

I can't.

I unwrap my Christmas presents like they might have the answer, or even a clue. I'm glad of the distraction. Emanuel, Detroit, they had dazzled me and left me totally starstruck. Boarding the flight, I was looking forward to coming home, but I was coming home to say goodbye. I could picture my new life in the Kronk. I knew I'd belong. But little doubts bred bigger ones, and now I don't know any more.

Gary and Billy are in contact regularly, to impress upon me that I still have another option. Fools rush in. I'm twenty-one and I have all the time in the world to turn pro. Emanuel's offer is a good one, they know, but I need to take care that I'm not blinded by the lights. If something doesn't feel right, for whatever reason, I shouldn't be afraid to wait.

The same offers will still be there or will come again. There might even be better ones. The pro game doesn't sleep on good boxers, they assure me.

A few weeks after Emanuel called me for the first time, I was back in training with the Irish team in the National Stadium. A package arrived for me, a big box, little gems of Americana in its stamps and stickers. There was a huddle, the rest of the team gathering around to take a look, enviously, as I ripped open this box of Kronk gear. A gorgeous red and gold varsity jacket with the Kronk logo stitched onto the front, and when I turned it over, my name on the back. Kronk T-shirts too, ANDY LEE in giant lettering.

Look at this stuff. You can't just walk into the shops and buy it. You have to earn it.

'Where did you get that from, Andy?'

'Emanuel Steward sent it to me. I was talking to him a few weeks ago. He wants me to turn pro.'

The lads all wanted to know the story, and I was happy to tell it. Billy brushed it off in two sentences.

'Did you see what I got, Billy?'

'Sure anyone can get a shirt printed with your name on it. What's the big deal about that?'

It brought me back down to earth with a bit of a bump, and I resented it. This was the Kronk Gym sending me clothes. Billy was a fighter himself, he knew what this meant. So what if he was right. He could have let me have my moment without taking the shine off it and trying to drag me down.

Financially, the Irish Amateur Boxing Association and the Irish Sports Council will never be able to match a consortium of American businessmen, but they want there to be no doubt about how much they want me to stay, and to see that they're going to their absolute limit to give me a genuine alternative. Irish boxing is on the verge of its next big breakthrough, the seeds sown by the High Performance Programme ready to blossom. But they need a leader, a captain, a poster boy for the next golden generation. They can't offer me any more than the max grant of €40,000 a year; that's set in stone. But every time we speak, they've wrangled another nice incentive to add to the package. There's a bonus for every major championship medal I win between now and the Beijing Olympics, and there'll be no shortage of opportunities there. An educational grant to support me going back to school, and then on to college. A sponsored car as well. I appreciate the lengths that they'll go to to back me.

I torment myself with the hypotheticals of both options, and the more I think about it, talk about it, the less certain I am. This brand-new world is stretched out in front of me, a vast expanse of the most amazing possibilities, but if I'm going in, I know I have to go in with my eyes open. Maybe Emanuel's right, maybe I will be a world champion within eighteen months. Maybe I'll be homesick, or I won't be able to hack it in Detroit. Maybe I'll lose. Maybe I'll end up broke or brain dead. I know that's my mam's fear. She brings it up sometimes, but frames it a bit more gently than that. She's right. It happens.

During one of our calls, Emanuel tries to reassure me that the pro game isn't this dangerous place that should be feared:

'Andy, after you come over here and make your debut, when you go back to Ireland, those people who are warning you not to turn pro, they'll be the very same people asking you to take photos and sign autographs.'

I'll risk it all by staying amateur, but even at that, it's a much smaller risk. I might not even qualify for Beijing, never mind win a medal, but there's also a lot more security. I won't need to uproot my whole life to move to the other side of the world, leaving behind my family and friends and the amazing woman I have just met and with whom I'm pretty sure I'm already falling in love. The money is good, and if it all goes to plan, I'll spend the next four years developing as a better and better boxer, winning medals and staying in the spotlight, attractive to sponsors, and at the end of it all, I'll still have the chance to turn pro. If I have an Olympic medal in my back pocket when the time comes, all the better.

I don't even get into the reasons with Damian for now. He doesn't try to change my mind or to convince me to do otherwise. I appreciate how much work he is after putting in on behalf of this kid he barely knows, but he is remarkably philosophical about the whole thing.

'Andy, that's absolutely fine, it's your decision. I'll call Emanuel to let him know and to say thanks.'

I don't speak to Emanuel myself, but I do call Tony Dunlop. He's livid, and he's not afraid to let me know.

'Andy, you're making a big, big mistake. You're making a huge mistake that you'll really regret if you don't take this opportunity.'

I don't get into a row. I stand my ground and explain to him that my mind's already made up, but when I hang up, it takes me a moment to gather my thoughts. I'm stunned. Our relationship is a fairly typical one for a fighter and a coach, respectful but not overly close. I was ringing him as a courtesy, not to ask for his advice. I hadn't expected him to question and undermine my decision like that. He had been in Detroit with me. Maybe he felt that I would be the one to open doors for him in America. What hurts me the most is that kernel of truth in what he is saying to me. That uncertainty, the possibility that in a year or two this decision will look like absolute lunacy, is there like a scab and he picks at it. Who are you, I think to myself – who are you to make me second-guess myself and feel bad about my decisions?

My next call is to Gary. 'I've made my mind up. I want to stay amateur. What do we need to do?'

It's four o'clock in the afternoon and he doesn't want to waste a moment.

'Can you be up in Dublin in the morning? I'll send out a few messages now and we'll have a press conference first thing tomorrow to announce it.'

I feel like asking what the rush is, but I say nothing. The papers know that this tug-of-war is ongoing, and that the deck is stacked in America's favour, so Gary wants to come out and declare his victory. A public announcement locks me in, like a vow on the altar. Once everyone has seen you stand up and say 'I do', signing the papers is just a formality. I go with the flow, tell Gary I'll be up tomorrow. I do the press conference, and say all the right things. Staying amateur is the right decision for me, as a boxer and as a person. I still want to be a professional world champion. I'm not giving up on that dream, but I'm staying here in Ireland to realise a bigger one. I have unfinished business. I want to win an Olympic gold medal for my country.

That should be it, the end of the worry, but the next few months feel like a lifetime. I go back to boxing. Go back to winning. A few weeks later, I win another national title, my third. I go to the Four Nations Tournament and win that too. After that I've two exhibition fights against one of the best amateur middleweights in the world, a Cuban, Yordanis Despaigne. He beats me in the first fight. When we meet again in the Stadium the following week, there's no way he's beating me twice.

And on the outside, everything seems rosy. Full steam ahead for the World Championships. But it's April, nearly three months since we made the announcement at that press conference, and I still haven't officially signed any contract. I'm going out training, fighting, winning in the Irish vest, upholding my end of the bargain, but their end of things still hasn't materialised. There are more discussions and negotiations and delays. I'm patient but the deal we discussed, the deal I thought we had agreed, still hasn't come together. Big promises cost nothing to make, but when the time comes to pull the trigger, there's only blanks in the chamber. They played their scare tactics about the pro game, convinced me that it was full of people who couldn't be trusted, but now that it has come to it, they are doing the exact same thing to me.

I thought I was being sensible by taking the safer option and staying amateur – the road more travelled – but I realise that's not going to fulfil me. I've made a mistake, and it chews me up. I ring Damian again to see what he thinks. Throughout all of this, and from this point on, he becomes one of my most trusted advisors, my cornerman outside the ring who always has my back. A close friend as well. I ask him, 'Can you get on to Emanuel and the guys in Chicago and see if we can get that deal back?'

He promises that he will, but we both know that these aren't the kind of people that hang around to be asked twice. We had our chance and I've blown it. Emanuel reassures me, tells me to stay patient, that we'll find a way. I'm Irish, I'm marketable, and I can fight. I'm an American dream.

I go down to the Stadium and meet Billy in the office. I tell him that I've changed my mind, and I'm upfront with him about my reasons: I don't want to be the guy who plays it safe and ends up with regrets. He respects my decision and doesn't try to talk me out of it. There's no more communication or negotiation after that; when I leave the Stadium that day, I leave the Irish amateur set-up as well.

I start travelling over and back to America regularly and spend more and more time with Emanuel. He invites me to Vitali Klitschko's training camp, where he's getting ready for his title defence against Hasim Rahman. He throws me in against the best middleweight there to see how my sparring's holding up. I'm well able for him. When I'm in Detroit, I stay in Emanuel's house. I have my own room. I'm in the Kronk every single day, in there with seasoned pros, pushing myself harder and harder. I might still be an amateur, but I want there to be no doubt that I'm the best amateur in the room.

Every time I speak to Damian, nothing has changed. Still no offer. He tells me to be patient, that the investors have other priorities and that it will take time. I call my mam. I need the chat.

'Are you sure you want to do this? You can stay here and you can have a good life for yourself. You could get a job in the IABA afterwards and you'll be set for life. You won't have to worry about anything.'

Everything she says is true and makes sense, and at the same time, it only makes me realise how much I value the alternative.

'You could be like Billy Walsh, Andy, do his job.'

'Mam, why would I want to be like Billy Walsh when I can be like Oscar De La Hoya?'

She knows that I've made my mind up, that I'm more sure than ever. I'm getting great experience in Detroit with Emanuel but to what end? Unless there's a contract there for me at the end of it all. I'm not getting any closer to an Olympic medal, or to a professional world title. I'm running to stand still. And unless there's an offer on the table soon, I'll have no option except to swallow my pride and go back to Gary.

I'm back in Dublin, sitting up late in Maud's parents' house, watching TV with her and her brother Luke. The fight's on. Wladimir Klitschko against Samuel Peter. We're messing about. Luke's a film maker, and he tapes us doing a mock interview. Soon I'll be doing these all the time. We laugh and we joke but once Maud has that remote control in her hand, her microphone, she asks the questions that she knows are on my mind.

'Do you find it slightly frustrating sitting here watching Sky Sports when you know you could be there yourself?'

'I know, yeah. I had hopes to be there but it wasn't meant to be, I guess.'

'Did you realise that big-money contracts like this could take so much time?'

'No. I mean, it doesn't have to have taken this long.'

Eventually, there's a breakthrough of sorts. Emanuel wants me to fly out to Chicago. The only time I've met these investors was a year ago, a flying hello-goodbye on the way to Vegas. They've never seen me train or spar, never seen me throw a punch in person. Emanuel's faith in me is gospel, but before we agree anything, they want to see what I can do for them.

I pull the collar of my jacket up around my face as far as it can go, anything to keep warm. Winter in Chicago is no joke. It's a beautiful city, full of life, but wherever they're taking me is anything but. The gym they've picked is not only rough around the edges, the rest of it is pretty rough too. It doesn't feel like the kind of place that has been home to too many new beginnings over the years.

They've picked the sparring partners. Partners, plural, three of them. I might tire but they'll be fresh. They might as well be licking their lips, ready to end a dream like their own was ended once upon a time. Pain shared is pain halved, or something like that. Perry, the investors, smile. If I'm as good as they've been led to believe, surely it doesn't matter who I spar. There's a bounty on my head, a cash prize, $500 I think, for whoever can knock me out. These boys are hungry.

They think it's a race, that whichever one of them gets the first shot at me will get the money. They don't realise that I'm a Kronk fighter in all but name. A Kronk fighter is not going to come to some little community club in Chicago and be intimidated. And he's certainly not going to lose. They have $500 at stake, but I have it all on the line.

They load up their big shots and they come at me. I slip and I counter like it's a Wednesday afternoon tune-up with my team-mates. Survival is not enough here. I need to impress, to make sure that there's no doubt in anyone's mind. I throw a combination. Jab. Right uppercut. Left hand. BANG. BANG. BANG. Emanuel explodes to life.

'That's it, that's it, that's it. Did you see what he just did there? That's it. You know that's it.'

It's a combination that he loves for southpaws. We've been drilling it, breaking down the technique, studying the angles, the impact, and now it's part of my arsenal, subconsciously, there for me when I need it. My opponent staggers, his head snapped back. Each element lands flush. Perfect 10s.

I get showered and changed, and they take me out to this big restaurant for lunch. Despite the back-and-forth of the negotiations, there's never any animosity between us. It's all business. We could talk all day, but we're talking about everything except my deal. It's written all over my face. It must be, because when I get tired of waiting and bring it up myself, nobody is surprised.

'Look, what's going on with the contract? Every time you ask for something, we give it to you, and then you come back and you're asking for something else again.'

The adrenaline is still pumping and I'm getting emotional.

'I just want to fight.'

I stop short of pleading with them, but now that they're sitting here, face-to-face with me, they're under no illusions.

'Fly back home to Ireland tomorrow. We'll have your contract over to you the next day.'

They're true to their word. The day after I get back, I meet my lawyer in Dublin. Everything is there, as we've agreed, and I sign the contract. I am a professional boxer.

I walk down George's Street hand-in-hand with Maud on Christmas Eve. It's perfect, and I fully intend to savour every moment of these next few weeks before I have to leave. We stop at the ATM as the crowds rush on around us. I enter my pin code and the two of us stand, staring, at the balance on the screen.

DETROIT

‹ ›

I can smell the smoke. It finds me in my room. Not the acrid, bitter kind that sticks in your throat and alerts you to danger: the type that makes you want to go to the source, not gather your belongings and run away to safety. So I go. Outside in the yard, Emanuel closes the lid on one smoker and gently opens another for inspection, savouring the middle act of his play of three acts. I observe. A slight rotation here. Another dab of sauce there, delivered with an artist's flick of the basting brush.

There must be enough ribs there to feed fifty people. I saw them last night, laid out in the kitchen for the opening act, a couple of weeks' worth of meat at a time, as Emanuel smothered them with his marinade recipe that people would kill for. Now the signal has gone out, can be smelled all over the neighbourhood, the prelude to the grand finale. Cancel the dinner plans. Emanuel's got ribs on.

They come, cars arriving in procession outside the house on Bretton Drive. Every phone conversation ends the same way: ribs in the yard tonight, you guys gotta come over and say hey. Invite or not, all are welcome. Straight off the barbecue, piled high on the plates, charred perfectly to the brown side of golden, the meat falling from the bone. Some stay for a while, catch up and chat on whatever makeshift seats they can find. People I know, and people that I don't yet. Others wrap their plates, say a quick thank you, and leave with their treasure trove. And Emanuel stays at the heart of it all, laughing, joking, tongs in his hand, doling out more food than any of these people could eat at their most hungry. Enjoying the company of his friends.

And when most of the ribs are eaten and the last of the crowd goes home, I'm already home. It was never my plan to live in Emanuel's house. It is only a temporary arrangement when I first come to Detroit, until I settle into this new city, find my feet and move into a place of my own. But every time I think about leaving, one of us finds a reason for me to stay until Emanuel's home becomes my home too.

I've stepped out of real life and into the heart of the boxing universe, and its soundtrack is a ringing phone. Emanuel has five at my last count, two mobiles and three landlines, and if he had the same amount again, they'd all be ringing constantly as well. His office is in the house; I know his assistant Lainey and his driver Charles from my first trips out to visit. But this office does not keep normal hours. I lie on my bed, watching TV, and I can hear Emanuel on the phone in his bedroom across the hall. Our doors are never closed. He finishes one call, and before the next one starts, he shouts across to fill me in. Hey, Andy, wait till you hear this. That was such and such. Guess what he said. Can you believe this? Can you believe that?

It's a promoter calling to negotiate. Bob Arum or Lou DiBella or Richard Schaefer. It's a reporter calling for a quick word, on or off the record. It's a boxer calling for advice. It's a call from down the street. It's a call from the other side of the world. He makes time for all of them, and if he misses a call, he'll call back. I'm beginning to understand how he ended up on the phone to me and to Damian in the first place. And with every name, there's a story to be told. Or an opinion. A caveat.

We sit and we watch TV together. Tapes of classic fights. Re-runs of whatever cards just took place the weekend gone by. He tells me his stories. He tells me the same ones over and over again, the way that middle-aged men who have lived extraordinary lives are prone to do sometimes. About Hearns, and Hagler, and The War. About the masterplan behind his first professional world champion, Hilmer Kenty, his eyes still holding the glint of a man who feels he's just got away with one and has nothing but pride for the artistry involved: how he flew to Puerto Rico and met with the guy pulling the strings on behalf of the WBA; how he promised a truckload of money that he didn't have to get a fight made against Ernesto España, their champion, and a little bit more money to get this relative novice bumped up the ratings to contender status; how he was up to his eyeballs in debt until he got a gift from the heavens when ABC's big televised card on the same night was cancelled, and they picked up España v Kenty instead; and how it was all worthwhile in the end because the Kronk had a world champion.

People come and people go in the house. Emanuel's brother James is living there when I first move in. His nephew Javan – everyone calls him Sugar Hill – stays sometimes, although he mainly lives in another of Emanuel's houses around the block. I meet Johnathon Banks, who has his own room in the basement. I met him once or twice when I was flying over and back, saw him in the gym, enough to know when I arrive that he's undefeated, 9–0, and The Next Big Thing for the Kronk.

My routine is the same every day. I get up at 7am and go for a run through the streets of Rosedale Park, the little neighbourhood that we live in about ten miles outside of downtown Detroit. It's pretty, even in the winter, with its old redbrick houses and big front lawns. It will never replace the Bog Road though. By the time my three or four miles are done, I've circled back to the house and I go out into the yard in the back for some shadow boxing before breakfast.

I shake off the snow from my runners and come back inside, and Emanuel is up and in the kitchen, getting some breakfast ready.

'I saw you out there shadow boxing this morning. Good job.'

Saw me on the security cameras, he means. The house is surrounded by them, as well as big electric gates. Everyone knows where he lives, so it would be an easy target if anyone was foolish enough to try it. It's another good reason why Emanuel likes having people living in the house with him as well.

If my alarm doesn't go off in the morning, or for some reason I decide not to get up for my 7am run, there's never a knock on the door from Emanuel. He's not that kind of trainer, and time has taught him that even if it provokes the desired response once, it's a waste of his time and energy in the long run. But he sees everything. Sometimes there's a little comment just to let you know he's watching, never to me, but to other fighters who stay with us from time to time. 'Oh, you must do your run in the afternoon, do you?', or 'Oh, yesterday's session must have been tough if you needed those extra hours in bed this morning.' He's willing to push, but he's always more interested in how far you are willing to push yourself.

And I'm willing. That insatiable work ethic was bred into me in my amateur days, and I'm not about to take my foot off the gas now. A lot of young European fighters have that drive too, but they don't have the pro-style technique of the Americans, the natural speed and technical gifts, the show-stopping flash. A hard-grafting European fighter with an American coach, or vice versa, a flashy American fighter with a European coach, that gives you the dream balance that you need. I see Johnathon Banks, how he's the number one in the gym, but he's not getting up and running in the morning. I'm not doing it to take his place, or to make him look bad, but when the time comes for Emanuel to go out for a meal or for a fight, I'm the one that gets the shout, not Johnathon.

From day one, he's educating me to be a champion. At least once or twice a month, he works for HBO television as the analyst for their boxing broadcasts, and every time he flies out to one of these big fight nights in Las Vegas or New York, he brings me with him. Charles drops us to the airport on a Thursday evening, and he's there again early on Sunday morning, ready to pick us up when we get in on the red-eye.

I'm in fighters' meetings, hanging around inside their dressing rooms, watching them as they get ready for these world title fights, to go out and realise their dream, or defend it, while millions of people watch, some hoping they fly and some hoping they fall. In Emanuel's eyes, it's a given that I will be on this stage myself soon, and this is all preparation: this is the hotel you'll stay in when you have a fight here; this is the room you'll be in; this is where you'll eat; this is what you'll eat. The first time I fight in Las Vegas, against Carl Cockerham, the first time I'm on a card in New York, against Dennis Sharpe, it all feels second nature to me. Nothing is unfamiliar.

Emanuel goes out of his way in those first few months to introduce me to Detroit, to show me this city that he adores, to make me feel at home. He brings me to Vicky's, his favourite rib shack in the city, and out to Cameron's, the steak house he loves in Birmingham. I see his celebrity for myself first-hand. He introduces me to Martha Reeves, the queen of Motown, a friend and a boxing fan. One of the first times my mam comes out to visit, we're walking through the mall and this big guy with a huge entourage and security detail calls out to us. Oh, hey, Andy, how you doing? My mam looks at me, totally puzzled.

'Who was that?'

'That's the mayor of Detroit, Mam. Kwame Kilpatrick. They call him the hip-hop mayor.'

The more time I spend with Emanuel, the more I come to see not only how much he is loved by the people in this city, but why they love him too. There's something magical, mystical about him that's very difficult to describe. Samuel Peter, the Nigerian heavyweight, comes closest to capturing it; he just calls Emanuel 'the Wizard Man'.

He is incredibly generous, with his time and with his knowledge. I watch him for days on end dealing with top promoters and high-powered lawyers, in person and on the phone, and then the next day he's every bit as comfortable stopping and chatting to a homeless person back in Detroit, giving them as much of his time if not more. Generous too, often to a fault, with his money. When the check comes, he's always the one to pick it up, no matter who else is sitting around the table. At Halloween, he brings me to Costco to help him, and he fills up his van with every different type of candy that money can buy. But only the good stuff.

'Where'd you get those? Put them back. Nobody wants those ones.'

And the line of kids stretches around the block all evening. The best sweets in town and the chance to say hi to Emanuel Steward is a combination that can't be beaten.

I see him stretch himself to breaking point at times, living from fight to fight, or pay cheque to pay cheque because he has over-extended himself. He makes sure his fighters have the best gear, no matter what the cost to him: the Kronk coats at $200, $300 a pop; the Mizuno boots, the best on the market, set him back $300 or $400 a pair. And the Kronk is not just a talent factory to him. It's a community, a family, and he knows that some people come through that door, and they will never be the stars of the show, but they couldn't get by from day to day without his help, and they're as welcome as the best fighter in the room.

He still makes room for his own flamboyant lifestyle: good food, sharp clothes, fast cars. The day his Rolls-Royce Corniche comes back from the garage, Emanuel parks it out on the lawn in the back garden. It is absolutely stunning, a beautiful candy-apple red, a classic. The iconic front grille, gleaming, freshly polished before it was returned from the shop in Arizona, whitewall tyres, and a convertible drop top. The kind of car that you would happily stand and admire all day and never need to drive.

I'm so enchanted by it that I offer to clean it. No small job on a blistering summer's day but I'm happy to do it, and I take my time over it. No spots, no streaks, making sure every last detail on it is perfect, down to the spokes of the wheels, until the sun is dancing off the polish. Emanuel is impressed.

'Nice job, nice job. When you come back from the gym later, we'll go and take it out for a drive, the two of us.'

There's no time for hanging around in the gym that day. I

get in, train hard, and get out. Emanuel's ready to go when I get home and has his heart set on a steak in Cameron's, four or five miles down the road. I sit into it, for real this time, and as Emanuel pulls out of the driveway, he puts his seatbelt on.

'Nobody is going to miss us driving this car down the street. We don't want to get stopped.'

We never usually wear seatbelts but Emanuel has the drop top down, enjoying the evening sun, and it's like a presidential parade as we cruise down Grand River Avenue. Everyone is waving, calling out to us.

'Emanuel, Emanuel! Hey, Emanuel, how you doing? Good fight the other night.'

And Emanuel is laughing and waving and throwing out little one-liners here and there. He's loving it, and I am too. As we pull on to the Southfield Freeway to head for Birmingham, I ring Maud.

'You'd want to see this car. It's Emanuel's old Rolls-Royce. It came back from the shop this morning. We're on our way to Cameron's now.'

We're doing fifty miles an hour on the freeway, maybe sixty, in no rush, enjoying the drive, when there's a loud bang. Emanuel loses control of the car and it starts spinning, spinning across the middle lane of the freeway.

'OH SHIT.'

We're dead. My phone flies out of my hand as we spin and slam headfirst into the separation barrier in the middle of the road.

'Emanuel, you OK?'

Somehow, thankfully, he's completely fine. The seatbelts – those seatbelts that we never wear – saved our lives. I'm bleeding. I smacked my head off the front dashboard on impact. I start to check to see where the blood is coming from, if one of the old cuts around my eyes has reopened, and then I realise that it's on my hand.

We sit there for a minute, in total shock. Nothing's broken. We're both OK. But when we get out to inspect the damage, it's not good. The car is destroyed, a total write-off. Bits of loose rubber are still attached to the front wheel rim. The guy in the shop had warned Emanuel that the tyres were worn, that they needed to be changed, but he didn't pay too much attention. Sure we're only going a few miles down the road and back, he thought, but it didn't take much for it to blow out. Incredibly, on the Southfield Freeway, which is usually bumper to bumper at 6pm, there weren't any cars near us when the tyre blew. We would have taken them out as well.

Now there's lots of cars passing us by as we stand around this wreck in the middle of the freeway. That's Emanuel Steward, that's Emanuel Steward! A TV truck pulls up a few minutes later, a reporter and a camera. They want this for tonight's news.

Emanuel phones his friend Wilcox to come and collect us. Wilcox is a mechanic. He takes one look at this beautiful Rolls-Royce and doesn't even need to say a word. We get into his car and we never see it again. The shock is starting to set in as we get back to the house. Emanuel must be devastated. I can't imagine how much the car cost him.

He looks at me.

'We're still going to Cameron's, right?'

And we do.

〈 〉

They say it's easier to leave than to say goodbye, but clichés weren't much consolation on the morning my dad dropped me out to Shannon Airport. The opportunity of a lifetime comes at a cost.

It's only been a few weeks but I miss them all. I'm excited to have them come to America, to show them my new life, and for them to share my professional debut with me. March 10th 2006 in the Joe Louis Arena, Detroit, I've a six-rounder against a Michigan kid named Anthony Cannon. Johnathon's fighting as well; we're listed as co-main events. My mam and my dad have flown out, and my uncle Johnny, my mam's brother, comes up to meet them from his home in North Carolina. Roger is here, and so is Maud's brother, Luke, who captures the whole week on camera. The first step on the journey.

Emanuel knows why they're here, knows they're curious, sceptical even, and he goes out of his way to make sure that they get the full VIP treatment. He puts them up in the house he owns around the corner, and invites them over so that they can see where I live. He brings them down to the Kronk, my second home. He takes us all out for meals and shows them the city at its best, but Detroit has a lot of scars and there's no way to cover them all.

My dad's not blown away by America, by Detroit. I can see it. He'd just as soon be back in Ireland where it's not so cold and not so grey. I love this city, love its proud people, but it has always been a place of extremes. 'Motor City', it hitched its star to the car industry and boomed, but it was a city divided long before the summer of 1967 when Detroit's forgotten black population said no more to segregation, discrimination, harassment, and racism. The riots. And when the jobs kept disappearing, so too did a lot of the rich white people. The famous Eight Mile Road sits as a line dividing the poor city and the wealthier suburbs, the haves and have nots. It's like night and day from one side of the street to the other. Now it's too big for the city that it has become, and when we drive downtown, the streets are lined with ghosts: shells of businesses that haven't been open in twenty years or more; estate after estate of abandoned, derelict houses. A city pockmarked by crime and unemployment. These people have had it tough, but they're still determined to put their best foot forward, to rise again.

I'm the white kid in a black city. The white kid in a black restaurant when we stop off in the Rosedale Café, not far from the house, on the way home from the gym, me, Johnathon, and Aaron Pryor Jr. It's a soul food or no food kind of place, and they introduce me to the best of it: chicken, greens, cornbread, grits.

You hear stories about how tough and dangerous it can be but I never feel unwelcome or unsafe in Detroit. I know where to go and where not to go. You stand out in a crowd but people are interested in you, in a good way. They want to know why you're here, if you like it. Being white is a shield in itself; nobody really wants to make trouble for you. Spending time with Johnathon and Aaron quickly opens my eyes to their reality. A few weeks after I move to Detroit, the three of us take a trip upstate to the Michigan Golden Gloves state championship. Ed Williams and Domonique Dolton, two more boxers from the gym, come with us, the five of us squeezed into Johnathon's car. Four black guys and a white guy. There's nothing much to look at out the window. The fields and farms of rural Michigan roll by. We head north along the freeway until the police lights flash in the rear-view mirror.

'What's going on? Why are we getting pulled over?'

We haven't been speeding and Johnathon's driving has been perfect. He gives me a tired look as he pulls over to the side of the road and rolls down the window. The police officer has a good look around, eyeballs us all, asks where we're going and what we're doing. Once we tell him our story and he sees the gym bags, he tells us we're free to go without so much as a word as to why we were stopped in the first place. And without any further explanation from the others, I know that stops like this aren't unusual: just one more insult that society expects them to sit there and silently tolerate. We get stopped by the police two more times before we get to the tournament, and three times on the way home.

We never have any trouble when we're with Emanuel or Sugar Hill. The Kronk is as much a part of Detroit's identity as the old Ford plant on the River Rouge or Berry Gordy's recording studio on Grand Boulevard. The red and gold jacket is a badge, an invitation to a city which has boxing in its blood to stop and talk to you.

'Hey, you're in the Kronk? Good job, good job. What's your name? When are you fighting? What weight are you at?'

There's a respect there, explicitly, for Emanuel, for the Kronk, and for what it represents. An understanding that it's a place where there are no reputations, where everybody is reaching for the next level, whatever that might be, and bringing each other on. Young kids and seasoned professionals training side by side. And if I'm good, there are a dozen others in there who know that they have to come up to my standard and meet me there because I sure as hell won't be coming back down to theirs. Once you walk through that door, everyone gets treated the same, whether you're a world champion or a one-fight amateur. It's a battle. You have to prove yourself. Bam makes sure of it.

When he was yelling 'fresh meat, fresh meat' at me on that first day that I came in to spar, I thought that I was being singled out, but that's just Bam's way. He brings the noise.

'You motherfucker. You ain't shit. You ain't shit. This is the Kronk. You're going to get your ass whooped today. Oh yes you will, boy.'

Bam's real name is Arthel Lawhorne. He was a cruiser-weight, heavyweight, during his own fighting days. A real game journeyman, the kind of guy who would take any fight on a day's notice, and couldn't care less about his record. A showman, King Bam they called him because he used to wear a crown down to the ring. He fought Ray Mercer back when Mercer was just starting out; Mercer had him out of there in a round and a bit. He's larger than life. It's all a bit of a performance, but it's a test as well, and you can see the guys who react. The tough guys take offence to being called out and get into the ring all fired up; other guys are totally psyched out and intimidated, and you can see them shrink before the first punch is thrown.

'Kid, you got a nickname yet?'

I don't. I'd thought about it a bit, and then I liked the idea of being the guy without a nickname. No nickname, no gimmicks, just boxing. They tell me I need a nickname though, mainly for Bam's benefit, it seems.

'PREEEEESENTING THE EIGHTH WONDER OF THE WORLD, ANDY SHARPSHOOTER LEE.'

It sticks for a couple of my early fights but never catches on. By the end of my career, I'm back to being Irish Andy Lee, plain and simple.

When my mam and my dad come down to see the gym, they can't get over the heat of the place, and they're just sitting there. It's packed, thirty people, fifty people, all working hard in this tiny space, but you never hear anyone complain about the heat. In fact, it's the opposite.

'Turn up the heat! Turn up the heat!'

If you hear that cry, that's when you know it's hot. It's our running joke, a little wry acknowledgement that it can't be avoided – small room, big crowd, old-school exposed heating pipes – but that part of it is by design as well. It's hot in winter but in the Detroit summer, with its heat and its humidity, it's hard to breathe. And that's a good thing. Making weight gets a whole lot easier when you're naturally sweating pounds of it out of you on a daily basis. And if you can train in these conditions, once you get into the arena on fight night, it will be like breathing fresh air.

The Kronk's greatness isn't something you read about in a history book. If you don't watch where you're walking, you'll bump into it while you're warming up. It's all around me. A man in dark glasses stands on the apron of the sparring ring and calls out words of encouragement to his son inside.

'It ain't Sugar Ray Leonard time, it ain't Joe Frazier time, it's your time.'

And you have to remind yourself that this man is quite possibly the best light-welterweight ever to lace up a pair of eight-ounces: Aaron Pryor, The Hawk himself.

You feel special just to be there, sharing this room with them, being a part of the environment that shaped them into the superstars that they were, and then you remind yourself that these guys have seen thousands of young fighters come through the door, tagging along behind Emanuel, and that Emanuel himself has probably proclaimed a significant number of them to be world-champions-in-waiting. They take an interest, they stop and they chat and they give you little bits of advice, pass on the tricks learned over a lifetime at the top, but at the end of it all, you're just another kid until you show them otherwise.

This is still their home. One day, a few years in, Tommy Hearns asks me to get in with him for a few rounds of sparring. He's maybe fifty years old, twice my age, and we both know that if I get in there with him, I'll go for it. That's what he wants but I can't bring myself to do it, to be in the ring punching a hero of mine, an idol. I don't want to make a fuss, so I just laugh it off.

'I can't today, Tommy. I'll get you again.'

Emanuel gives me all of the time I need, and I'm the perfect student for him. Everything he teaches me is canon; everything he promises me, I believe. I get to know the little quirks of how he likes to do things and they become an unspoken part of our routine, why he likes to sit down when he's wrapping his fighters' hands, or why he likes to use cocoa butter and not Vaseline on their faces before they get into the ring. He tells me: Vaseline is petroleum, it's a chemical, and you don't want that on your skin, but cocoa butter softens the skin and it deflects the punches. And, he fails to mention, it smells good too.

He's obsessive about the clothes we wear in the ring.

Emanuel explains that he wants his fighters in bright colours because when tribes were going to war in the jungle, bright colours gave them more energy and made them feel more aggressive. The colour white makes you feel lighter, so he insists that we all wear white Mizuno boots and white socks. Even in the gym, the colours are always bright because darker colours, they're dead, there's no life in them, they don't give off the same energy. When I fight, I wear red velvet shorts with a gold trim, my name on the waistband across the top, and the Kronk logo on the leg. I switch to the traditional Kronk shorts, the famous gold, for one or two fights over the years as well.

At any given moment in the Kronk, if you stop for a second and just observe, there's a lesson there to be learned. Emanuel won't ever try to change a fighter from his natural style, to apply some one-size-fits-all philosophy of what a championship fighter should look like and try to force a square peg into a round hole. Emanuel's way is more like an identikit: he takes whatever strengths a fighter brings in the door and tinkers with it, working to refine the core elements that he really values. Balance and rhythm.

I don't even see myself change. I was always a boxer, a counterpuncher, as an amateur, and my footwork was one of my strengths, but when I look back on the tapes after working with Emanuel for a while, I can see a huge trans-formation. I'm boxing with much more authority, and I'm much more composed. I've thrown off the shackles of that amateur style where the priority is to land a punch, even if it's only a tap, and avoid one in return. It's all in the moment, and you have to act and react to your situation quickly, because it's a short fight and time is against you. In the pros, you can afford to take a few punches if it carves out the opportunity for you to land your big one. I learn to be patient, to pace the fight and to plan ahead, to think beyond the next exchange.

Emanuel watches me, gets a sense of the combinations that I naturally lean towards, and then adds a few little flourishes of his own.

'Here, try this. Just jab, jab, same pace, same power … and then BANG.'

He teaches me punches that he knows my opponents won't see: throw the exact same jab consistently, let them get used to seeing it in a certain rhythm, let them think that they've established a pattern and then, just as they get comfortable, let your left hand go at a different speed and different power to catch them off guard. He pulls the pads on to drill me in an old Tommy Hearns move: throw your short combos in the usual rhythm, one-two, one-two, one-two, but then let your jab linger for a split second longer, one-pause instead of one-two, so that your glove sits over your opponent's eye for the briefest of moments, a half a beat, and obscures their vision. And then hit them with the two to end all twos. They won't see it coming.

He asks Milton McCrory to train me for one of my early fights, and Milton has the same arsenal of tricks up his sleeve that he picked up from Emanuel twenty-five years earlier.

'Come here, let me show you this. It's called the Suzie Q.'

Rocky Marciano called his killer punch the Suzie Q, a short right cross amped up to eleven, but this is different. A Kronk special, perfect for a tall fighter like me to make the most of my reach advantage. Milton shows me: establish a distance that works for you, keep it constant, lay the trap, and then when your opponent makes his move, take a little step back. He'll miss, but he'll still be in range and wide open for you to throw your left. It's all about getting the timing right. No wonder it takes its name from a dance move.

And all of these little techniques, honed over hours in the gym, they're all geared towards finding the knockout, because that's how Kronk fighters win. It's more exciting, it's more attractive, it's more dominant, and it's the golden rule of Emanuel's fight philosophy, the thing he takes most pride in. Work the opening. Find the punch. Finish the fight.

I go the distance against Anthony Cannon that first night in the Joe Louis Arena. I win a clear decision at the end of six rounds, and then go out to celebrate my first professional victory with my family and friends. There's no knockout but there's no rush. I'm just getting started.

‹ ›

Roger racks the balls, picks up the cue, and breaks. I'll never hear the end of it if I let him beat me. It used to be computer games when we were younger, now it's pool, entire evenings lost while we play on the table that Emanuel has down in the basement.

I love being in Detroit. I love the opportunity. I know it's where I have to be to do what I want to do, but that doesn't mean it's not difficult. The wide eyes and the buzz last for a few weeks, but once I settle in, the adventure becomes life. I'm thousands of miles away from home, from my friends, from my family, from Maud. During the week I have my routine, but the weekends can be lonely. Sunday is always a quiet day. I get up early and watch whatever English football they're showing on TV, but there's not much else. I read Viktor Frankl's book, *Man's Search for Meaning*, and come across his theory of 'Sunday neurosis': that feeling of emptiness that people get when their hectic life slows down at the weekend. That's me. I love Monday mornings and getting right back into it – I'm training, I'm fighting, I'm busy. Emanuel lets me know that if I'd like some company, Roger is welcome to come and visit, that there'll always be room for him and he can stay with us for as long as he likes. Before long, he's living out here in Emanuel's house with me. I need him here. Over the years, he gets more and more involved helping out around the gym, and in my training as well. He's part of the team.

It's hard to make friends in boxing. Not hard to be friendly, or to have companions, but hard to make friendships that

113

last. I've always found that. I'd be in amateur squads with the same guys and get to know them for a year or two, but then they'd drop off, or get beaten, and somebody else would come in to replace them. I travel to different parts of America as a pro for training camps and I meet boxers, great people, that become very close friends for the two or three months that we're there. Maud hears all of these stories about these guys, the things we do together and the fun we're having, and then she never hears about them again. Once the camp is over and we go our separate ways, we don't keep in touch. We just accept that that's the way it is in boxing: short and intense. Fighters, friends, they come and go.

I get to know my team-mates in the Kronk – Johnathon, Aaron, Kermit Cintron. We're with each other every day, training, sparring, driving each other on. It's an intense atmosphere to get to know someone in, crackling with testosterone and tension. The emotions are extreme, and we all see each other at our best and our worst as well as every point in between. There's a certain type of bond that develops, an understanding that you're all riding the same rollercoaster, sharing the same pain and suffering together for the same reasons. The four of us spend a lot of time travelling together, in training camps or working each other's corners for fights. We talk about boxing, training, and our careers, but when I really need to talk to someone about a problem, I turn to Roger or Maud or my uncle Johnny, or ring home, or I deal with it by myself. We just don't have that kind of relationship. You want your team-mates to be people who will push you, not be your psychologists.

The first training camp I ever go to is in Mallorca. I watch the two boxers sparring in the ring and try to stay loose. I'll be the one in there in a few minutes, and Wladimir Klitschko is a big man. It was only a few months ago that I was sitting with Maud and Luke watching him win his world title eliminator. Now I'm part of his training camp for the title fight, I've a fight of my own on his undercard, and Emanuel wants me in there to spar against all 6'6", 240lbs of him. He's done his heavy lifting for the day, his power sparring, by the time I get in. Now he wants to work on his speed. He's obsessed with speed. When we're done, I hear him ask Emanuel: 'How was that? Was I OK today or was I slow?'

It's a real thrill to be in there with Wladimir. Sparring two rounds against him is like sparring seven or eight against a middleweight. It's physically exhausting just to try to get past his tree-trunk arms, and if you manage that, then you can start thinking about trying to actually hit him. I'm tall enough and fast enough to handle myself – I do OK most of the time – but he never goes out of his way to hit me hard. He likes sparring against me, thinks it's a good drill, and we do it a lot over the years. It gets harder and harder as the years go on because he gets better and better. I see that evolution right in front of my eyes, the way he's tailoring his training, all the little changes that he's making.

I catch him cleanly with a punch once, about a year after that first session, and he makes sure I know all about it. He hits me with a big shot to the side of the head, right on the ear, but I shake it off and we touch gloves at the end of the spar. I feel fine until I get back to my room and lie down, and the entire room starts spinning. The only way to stop it is to sit back upright again. I tilt my head to the left, and everything starts spinning again. I peel myself up off the bed slowly and go to find Wladimir's physio, ask him to take a look at it, but he can't see anything wrong. Whatever way the shot landed, it must have disrupted my balance and my equilibrium. I keep it to myself, and by the time I fight a few weeks later, it's all back to normal. But it teaches me a lesson about tagging the world heavyweight champion in sparring. As a middleweight, sometimes you've got to take a punch to throw a punch, but those rules don't apply to Wladimir. Big crowds come to watch him spar at his open workouts over the years, and he definitely doesn't want them to see me hitting him. He doesn't like getting hit, full stop. I realise that I need to use my feint a bit more when I'm in there, and by the end, I'm able to last four rounds against him.

The more time I spend with Emanuel, the more I learn about the unique way his mind works. On the final day of that first camp in Mallorca, he calls me into the gym and tells me that he needs my help. It will only take a minute. He passes me the end of a roll of hand-wrapping tape.

'Hold that there for me please, right up in the corner of the ring.'

I watch him pace across the side of the ring, corner to corner, making little marks on the tape as he goes, until he has done the same for all four sides. He doesn't explain why he's measuring our training ring or what he's trying to figure out. He just takes the tape back from me, cuts it, folds it in half so the two sticky sides touch each other, wraps it up and puts it in his bag.

'Thanks, Andy.'

I never quite figure out how Emanuel anticipated what would happen next. When we arrive in Mannheim for Wladimir's world title fight, we land right into the eye of a storm. On the day of the weigh-in, there's a huge dispute about the size of the ring. Don King is promoting Chris Byrd, Wladimir's opponent, and he's insistent that the fight will be cancelled if anything about the ring is changed at this late stage. The tension starts to cool off when Emanuel arrives. He doesn't need to command respect; he just gets it. Bernd Boente, Wladimir's manager, tells him what's going on. Emanuel goes to check the ring for himself and pulls the folded-up piece of tape out of his bag. The ring looks small, swallowed up in the middle of this big arena, but when he stretches the tape back out again, it matches up to the inch – the exact same size as the ring we had been using in Mallorca. He tells Bernd and Wladimir not to worry, that nothing needs to be changed. The next night, I open the card with a stoppage win against Wassim Khalil and then watch as Wladimir knocks Byrd out to become the heavyweight champion of the world.

I learn a lot from watching Wladimir as a young pro. The stereotype is that heavyweights are notoriously lazy in training but Wladimir is switched on from the moment he arrives into camp and outworks everyone there. He's sponsored by Mercedes, by Hugo Boss, he's a multi-millionaire, but there's no superstar arrogance. A model professional. Once or twice during a camp, he takes everybody out for sushi and relaxes a bit, but for the most part he keeps himself to himself, occasionally stopping for a polite chat, but never anything less than completely focused on the task at hand.

I'm always very grateful to be invited to his camps, and I don't want to do anything to lose that privilege. I keep my head down, train hard, and speak when I'm spoken to. Wladimir's one of the biggest names in boxing, and I'm a kid just starting out, but we slowly get to know each other. At one camp in Austria, I mention to him in passing that I play a bit of guitar.

'I have drums and a guitar in the place where I'm staying. Come up later.'

He picks me up and we go up to the cabin that he is staying in. He is just learning how to play the drums, and the two of us spend a couple of hours there, making small talk and jamming away. Our band needs a name; we call ourselves The Klits.

We bond more over music than we do over boxing. Wladimir usually arrives into the gym just as I'm finishing up my own session. I have the music blaring, and before he changes over to his own playlist, he asks me what we're listening to. Kings of Leon, 'Closer', I tell him. A good while later, I'm in New York with Maud, setting up a few bits in Trader Joe's, when the phone rings. I don't recognise the number, a +49 one from Germany. It could be anybody so I don't answer. When I get back to the apartment, the same number rings again and I pick up.

'Andy, it's Wladimir. How are you?'

'Hey, Wladimir, what's up?'

'I'm good, I'm good. I've somebody here who wants to talk to you.'

I recognise the voice as soon as Wladimir hands over the phone.

'Hey, man, how you doing?'

I play it cool, as though I regularly get calls from Caleb Followill, the frontman of Kings of Leon, and we chat to each other all the time. We talk about the show that they played in Cleveland not that long before. I drove down with Sugar Hill to see them, and we ended up staying in the same hotel and meeting them that night. Caleb remembers us alright; the rowdy boxing lads were hard to miss.

Maud stands there listening to one half of this conversation. She likes to remind me about how I did my best to keep it together while I was on the phone, and then jumped up and down around the room like an excited child as soon as we hung up. I always know now when Kings of Leon are touring in Wladimir's part of the world. He never forgets to call and say hi.

‹ ›

I didn't hear Jake LaMotta say it, but I was certainly starting to believe the hype: when I landed the punch that knocked out Carl Daniels, the lights went out on Broadway.

Up until that night, my first year in Detroit was a little bit of a runaway train, fast and frantic, with eight fights, eight wins, five of those stoppages. The buzz – who I was, where I'd come from, and what I could go on to do – picked up speed sooner than I might have expected, but pumping the brakes would do no good so the only real option was to strap in and try to enjoy the ride. And I did.

After winning my first two fights, I feel that I'm already doing enough to establish that I'm more than just another Kronk kid. People are starting to notice me, and I'm starting to notice them notice me. Emanuel introduces me to Jermain Taylor, middleweight champion of the world. Undefeated. Undisputed.

'Jermain is going to be training with me from now on, Andy. We'll get you guys to do some sparring.'

Taylor's first fight under Emanuel is a title defence against Winky Wright in June 2006, and I'm lined up to have my next fight that weekend as well. Keep learning, keep building, keep the momentum going. Nobody's thumbing through Taylor's CV in admiration when we get in for our first spar that day. He's fresh meat, just like anyone else who walks through that door. You say you're the best. Prove it.

I'm not going to be used as anyone's sacrificial lamb. There's a direct trade-off. If I show him respect, I'll lose it myself from the fighters who have stopped and are watching us now as we come together for the first time. His jab arrives like a warning: this ain't no game, kid, don't mess with me. But the room is on my side.

'Let's go, Andy. He's in the Kronk now.'

I can't be too bull-headed but I'm not going to shy away either. There's a whip to my punches that you wouldn't see in every sparring session. When he wants to get to it, I stand my ground, I give as good as I get. Afterwards, Emanuel tells him: you might be the undisputed middleweight champion of the world, but Andy Lee is the middleweight champion of this gym. This is his turf. You won't get nothing easy.

When we spar again a few days later, there's a real edge to it. I threw down the gauntlet on day one; now Taylor's ready to run it. Two fights into my pro career, the opportunity to pit myself against the man who just beat Bernard Hopkins is a great barometer for me to see where I want to be. A small part of me starts to think that I'm already getting there.

I fight the night before Taylor's world title defence in Memphis, across the road from the arena in a small little outdoor stadium on Beale Street. It's meant to be my TV debut, on one of ESPN's channels. They're pushing hard for my fight to be shown. Dan Rafael, their top boxing guy, is telling them they've got to show it. But the promoter is a local guy called Brian Young and he's not letting any of his fighters get bumped out of a TV slot so that they can show me instead. They put me on as the last fight of the night, after the broadcast is finished.

I get there early. It's a warm night in Tennessee, far too warm for me to be in the shoebox dressing room they've assigned me, so I spend the early part of the card sitting outside, waiting and waiting and waiting with the crowd's reactions as my commentary. The instantaneous roar that greets a good punch. The more sustained encouragement, on their feet, as a home fighter turns the screw. People see me sitting there and come over.

'You're Emanuel's kid. What time are you in at?'

A Kronk prospect is worth waiting for so some of the crowd, and most of the press people, stick around after the main event to watch me against Rodney Freeman, a young fighter from just outside the city. He's 5'6", and he's about to quickly find out that we're on different planets. About a minute in, he steps into me and throws a right hook, and I counter with a hard left straight down the middle, right on the button of his chin. Flattened. He somehow gets back to his feet, but his brain and his legs aren't on speaking terms right this minute. He wobbles. The referee has no choice.

Two-fight pros don't knock other kids out like that. Andy Lee is a blue-chip middleweight prospect, Dan Rafael writes, the kind of praise that is reserved only for the highest of the high. The phone starts to ring a bit more often. Emanuel is the master. He keeps a lid on any sort of loose excitement – Andy's still learning, he's got all the time in the world, what's the rush – but he knows that talk and profile are currency in this game, and even if he's out there publicly reining it all back in, every time he does it, another new person hears the name Andy Lee for the first time.

Bob Arum calls Emanuel to see if they can strike a deal for him to become my promoter. We discuss it. Emanuel looks after so many boxers on so many cards, he's got tremendous leverage when it comes to placing his fighters. That's how he was able to insist on the opening slot for me on Wladimir's bill in Mannheim in only my second fight, and how he tied my third fight into Taylor's title defence. But Arum and Top Rank Boxing are one of the biggest names in the business, and if Emanuel is able to open doors for me, Top Rank can kick them down.

We agree to a deal in the short term, three fights to begin with while we discuss the possibility of a more formal partnership. It's exciting. They want to start me in Las Vegas, on the undercard of the heavyweight title fight between Hasim Rahman and Oleg Maskaev, but that plan falls through and instead I fight a few days earlier in a much smaller Vegas venue.

I get my three fights with Top Rank, as promised, before it all goes cold. They're happy to deal with Emanuel, and he's happy that the contract they're proposing is a good one for me, for my development. It should be that simple but it never is. As soon as the Chicago investors get wind that there's a promotional deal in the pipeline, they insist on having their say. They put up the money for my signing fee, they cover my expenses to go to all of these training camps, so they should be the ones negotiating any deal. They're big businessmen, top lawyers, and they're used to having things their way. They don't see eye-to-eye with Emanuel on the details of the contract and they try to sideline him: we control Andy Lee; you're just the trainer; we'll do the negotiating. Too many cooks, too many conflicting interests, and ultimately, too much hassle for Top Rank. After the three fights, they walk away. I'm the one that suffers.

I don't let it get me down. Part of me knows that Top Rank match their prospects hard. The three guys they put me in against – Carl Cockerham, Jess Salway, and Arturo

Ortega – are beatable but they're no punching bags. But Emanuel doesn't let me have it any easier when he's matching me. Your talent dictates the pace that you can be moved at, he tells me. He has that old-school disdain for padding out a young fighter's record with walkover wins against tomato cans. He's not tossing me into fights I'm going to lose, sink or swim, but he wants my wins to mean something. An opponent with a winning record, but who will never be able to live with my style. Or try to catch a big name when he's on the slide. The first time I step up to eight rounds it's against Carl Daniels, a legit former world champion, but he hasn't been at his peak for a few years now. The stamina of going the extra rounds would be enough of a test for one night, but an opponent of Daniels's class, he's the kind of gate-keeper that will show the boxing world if I'm the real deal or if it's all just smoke and mirrors.

This is no time to slip. The fight has been sold out for weeks, five thousand tickets gone in a flash. Beg, borrow, steal, whatever; you still won't get into the Theatre at Madison Square Garden. It's the night before St Patrick's Day 2007, a card packed full of Irish fighters. Henry Coyle. The Clancy brothers from Clare, James and Mark. John Duddy as the headliner. And me against Daniels. I've done my bit to sell the tickets. My mam and my dad have flown over, as well as Ned and all of his family, and a few of my cousins. Damian is here with his wife, Linda, and Tony Dunlop is too. Emanuel's not there – he's in Vegas with HBO for Marquez against Barrera – but he sends Sugar Hill to look after everything and run the corner.

I'm coming in hot – getting a lot of buzz and attention – and the promoter doesn't like it. He's got connections to the

Duddy camp, and I get the feeling they wouldn't exactly be disappointed if my fight fell through.

When Daniels shows up heavy on the day of the weigh-in, it looks like they've got their wish. It's booked as a middleweight fight, a 160lbs limit, but Daniels is nowhere near it. I come in a pound under, and then there's consternation when he tips the scales at 170lbs. The fight's off, the fight's off, these guys can't fight – and they're right. There's no way that the commission can sanction a fight between the two of us with that much of a weight gap. If we can make it so that there's no more than seven pounds between us within the next hour, they'll sign off. Otherwise, forget about it.

Daniels wants the fight. He wants to get paid. The clock's already ticking. I check with the commission: 'Don't take my official weight yet. Can I reweigh in an hour when he's being weighed?'

I sprint across the road to the Tick Tock Diner on the corner of Eighth Avenue and grab the menu. The greasier the burger, the better. A large plate of fries as well, just to be sure, and wash it down with a milkshake as well for good measure. When I get back, Daniels is still there with Damian and Tony Dunlop, dressed in every bit of sweat gear they can find, doing shuttle runs up and down the steps of the theatre.

He's sweated out a couple of pounds, I've put on more than you'd think possible in the space of a few minutes, and we make it. The fight's on.

And now I'm standing in my corner, hearing Daniels's record for the very first time, with a little flash of doubt in my mind.

And in the blue corner, with a record of forty-nine wins, ten losses and one draw, thirty-one of those wins by way of knockout …

That's a lot of wins. That's a lot of knockouts.

The crowd get restless quickly in those early rounds. It's a Duddy crowd. They're used to seeing blood and guts, watching their man go to war, and now they're being served up the exact opposite as their appetiser. A close fight, very technical, and by no means a slugfest. The Irish guy is winning the rounds, but that's not enough to keep people happy.

Right hook to the body, that's my punch. All night. Daniels is a southpaw too, so I know it will land. I work it, let him know that he might be the one with the big record but I'll be the one dictating in here tonight. Midway through the second round, he realises what's happening, starts to see the hook coming, tucks in tight to catch it and counters with a right hook of his own.

The wheels start turning, but it takes me a minute to work out what's changed, what he's doing, and what I need to do next. Daniels takes his opportunity, and towards the end of the third, he catches me with a right hook of his own. It's a warning sign. Barry McGuigan is on commentary and he calls it: *Keep the fight at long range, get the shots off early, move the legs.* This is not the kind of guy you want to mix it with.

I go to throw the right hook again, and in the blink of an eye, I see it all so clearly. Daniels goes to catch and counter, and before he knows it, I've pulled back and turned that body shot into the most devastating right hook on the chin. A show stopper. He goes straight to sleep. I know it, and I'm walking away with my arm raised before he hits the canvas. Seven fights; seven wins.

Lights out on Broadway.

‹ ›

'**D**EEEEETROIT CITY!'
Johnny is the uncle that you hear before you see, a giant tricolour draped over his shoulders – BEST OF LUCK, ANDY – just in case there's any confusion about where he's from and who he's there to support. His accent has been diluted a bit by the years in America but the rest of him is as unmistakably Irish as ever: the pale skin, the thinning red hair, the endless chat, the mischievous glint, and the want for a bit of messing, the more childish the better. There's always messing when Johnny's around.

Charlotte, North Carolina, is a regular stopover point when I'm travelling back and forth across the country with Emanuel to fights and to camps. It becomes part of my routine to stay for a day, to go and see Johnny and his family. He's my mam's brother but moved to the States when he was younger, fell in love, and married an American woman, Kristen, and they have three children: Thomas, Ronan, and Niall. When I first move out to Detroit, I see Johnny every couple of weeks. He's there with my mam and my dad the night I make my debut, he travels across to Memphis when I'm fighting Freeman, and he flies out to Vegas in August and September to watch me against Cockerham and Salway.

He was always the American uncle when we were growing up but now I get to know him better than ever before. He rings me every couple of days for no real reason, just to see how I'm doing, what life's like in Detroit, how I'm settling in. For him, having me and Roger out in America feels like a little bit of home, a way for him to reconnect with Ireland,

and it's a little bit of home for me too in those first few months when life is still so new and different. He's someone who I can talk to, someone who I'm comfortable telling how I'm feeling. He'd find a way to ask, even if I wasn't volunteering the information, and I know that if it ever came to it and I needed him for any reason, he's only an hour and a half away on the plane.

When we fly out to those two fights in Vegas, everybody with us either has a job to do, or is in it for themselves and looking to get something out of it. Not Johnny. He's there because he's family, and because he wants to spend a couple of days with me and Roger.

'Don't bother booking a hotel, Johnny. Me and Roger have a room between us, and there's space for you here too.'

There's never any fuss with Johnny. He shares our room and he becomes part of the fight week camp, an extra pair of hands when we need them. He's in the gym when we're working out, filling the moments between drills, chatting away to Emanuel or Sugar Hill or Aaron or Johnathon, getting to know them too.

The Dennis Sharpe fight that November is my first time fighting in New York, in Madison Square Garden no less. The perfect excuse for all of the family and extended family to make a trip of it, as if the lack of excuse was something that would ever stop them. Maud is there with all of her family. My mam and my dad are there, and so are Dawn and Hayley, my sisters. I'm in fight mode, but for the rest of them, there's a party every night. They show me the photos and tell me how much fun I've missed. It's Johnny's first time to meet Maud and he sees it instantly. Before he flies home that weekend, he tells me she's a really lovely girl. There's an intent in the fact that he'd even say it, and it's enough to get the message across: look after her, you've done very well to find a woman like her.

He calls me again a week or two later and we live through it all again, the little stories that I haven't heard yet and the jokes that he forgot to tell me. He reminds me again how great Maud is. He asks how Emanuel's doing, starts thinking out loud about the entourage that seems to attach itself to him everywhere he goes and expects him to open his wallet every time. He's concerned about him. It's a run of the mill chat, same as any other week. You don't know at the time that it's the last time you'll ever speak.

———

Ed Williams, my team-mate from the Kronk, is with me in the car and we're on our way home from training. The phone rings as we're on the freeway. It's Kristen, which is unusual. She would never normally call me.

'Andy, there's been an accident. Johnny had a fall at work. He's in the hospital and he's not doing too well.'

I pull over onto the hard shoulder and stop so that I can understand what she's trying to say to me.

'What's going on, Kristen? Is Johnny OK?'

The detail of her words passes me by in a blur. I know instantly that it's bad. The doctors are with him in intensive care. Johnny's sleeping. In a coma. They're doing everything they can for him. Kristen has already spoken to my mam and her sisters. They're flying out today.

I tell Ed that I need to get back to the house. I don't know what I'll do when I get there. I only spoke to Johnny last week. Doctors have to be cautious. Maybe Kristen will ring back in a few minutes with better news. Maybe it will be OK. Maybe he'll be in Vegas with me and Roger again in a few weeks' time, same as always, ready for the fight and the pint afterwards. Maybe.

I have a flight to Charlotte booked and my bag packed before I know where I am. Sugar Hill arrives home. He knows Johnny. Everyone does. Johnny stayed in his house the first time he came out to Detroit. I try to explain but I'm not making sense. Leaving out details, the most important ones, deliberately. I need a lift to the airport. Sugar Hill will drop me there on the way to the gym. I'm in the front. The Romanian twins are in the back, the young lads that he is bringing up to the gym, Jacob and Joseph Bonas. A little diversion, a road trip on their way to training. I don't say a word the whole way there. They're laughing, messing around in the back with their other friend. They don't understand what's going on. How could they? I don't even understand, and what I do, I can hardly articulate. As we get closer to the airport, Sugar Hill asks me again before I get out of the car.

'Are you alright, Andy? What's going on? Is Johnny alright? Is he going to be OK?'

I don't even try to stop the tears. They've been coming for an hour now. I don't know. I don't know. I don't know.

When I get to Charlotte, I call Kristen to find out where he is, where to go. Johnny's still asleep when I get to the hospital, and I find a space among the tubes and machines to sit with him. I know what I'm looking at, but it's impossible to make sense of it, to relate it to the Johnny I know and the explanation I'm being given about how this has all happened. He wouldn't fall from a ladder and hit his head. He was born to be a builder. He lived his life on ladders, floated across beams and girders, every day since he was a young man. I spend the night beside him in hospital, watching the flashing screens on the life support machines, willing them to reveal some miracle; trying to be strong for Kristen, trying not to think about their three kids, my three young cousins, at home. I stay there and I talk to him, praying that he'll hear my voice and wake up and laugh. I wipe his mouth clean.

In the morning, the doctors make sure that we're comfortable, that we have everything we need, that we understand Johnny's situation. We wait, hoping that my mam and her sisters will walk through the door and have a chance to say their goodbyes, but Johnny goes in his own way, in his own time. I break down in tears again when my mam comes in a few minutes later. I hug her tight and don't want to let her go.

Johnny's friends come to a memorial service in North Carolina before we fly his body home to Limerick. I never liked funerals; I always thought that when my time came, it would be nice if I could just go, and be gone, and not have this sad occasion that everyone is obliged to come to when they're already suffering enough with their loss. But bringing Johnny home made me realise how important these traditions are, that the uniqueness of a life deserves more than tears. The grief and sadness stays with you for a long time, part of it stays with you forever, but those days give you important moments that live on as well and bring comfort as you celebrate the loved one to whom you're saying goodbye.

I go back to Vegas a few weeks later, to the same hotel, to what feels like the same room. I walk into it and I think

Johnny should be there, flicking through the channels, waiting for us to come back in. I turn the TV on but it's still as quiet as before. I go for dinner and remember what he ordered, think about the laugh we had that night. I walk into the arena and I think about where he would have been sitting.

Arturo Ortega is a fighter that you wouldn't want to take lightly: small, tough, the kind of guy that will hang in there all day, soaking up punches and coming forward to see what you've got next. He hasn't got much of his own to trouble me, but it's easy to see why he's never been stopped before. I'm drifting through the rounds, winning them, but just going through the motions.

Emanuel tells me to pick up the pace ahead of the final round, finish it off. I stand up off my stool and as I come out of the corner, all I can think is: Johnny. Whatever it means, wherever it comes from, in that moment I realise that he's still there with me, and things will be OK. I walk Ortega down and let my hands go, the punches landing in quick succession. His corner throw in the towel, and the fight is stopped.

Months later, I'm checking the voicemails on my phone, and it starts playing through some old messages that were never deleted. There's one from Johnny, just calling to say hi and see how things are going. I keep that old phone for years, and every so often, I take it out of the drawer just to listen to the voicemail, just to hear his voice again.

They live in a different world, the journeymen. They're part of a different sport. They don't come here to win. They come here to survive.

They know each other, share the same dressing rooms with the same faces week after week. United in the camaraderie of grim acceptance, bonded by the same bleak fate. Fed to a young prospect, eager to impress, so that he can get rounds under his belt and a win on his record. Or fed to each other by heartless promoters with no concern other than how they are going to pad out space on the card. Only the venues and the opponents change.

I hear them talking about the last fight. The last beating. If they got knocked down or were stopped standing up. If they made it to the bell, the biggest prize of all. Fighters who make it through without being knocked out can come back and fight again next week. Losing on points is practically a victory. Another cheque to take home, carved up by tax and doctors' fees and every other expense until it's whittled away to practically nothing.

I wonder if they loved it once, if this was their dream. If they were stars on the rise, the next big thing. I wonder what happened. I can see the ones who used to believe, who still feel that they're just a couple of good performances away from turning it around, who haven't made peace with a life of weekly or fortnightly losses. I can see it in their performances.

Clinton Bonds, a guy with four wins and eight losses, shows me a photo of his kids after we fight in the New Daisy Theatre in Memphis.

'I'm just doing this for them. I'm doing it for my kids.'

I'm not sure how much he got paid to take the fight against me, next to nothing anyway, maybe $500 before all of the deductions. I give him another $100 out of my cut.

'Here, you should buy something for your kids.'

You learn how to read these guys. You watch how they arrive. Does he look like he is just here for the trip? Does he look like he's just here for the payday? Does he have a team with him – a coach, a cutman – or is he here by himself? At the weigh-in, what is he drinking? What is he eating? Has he got his licence in order? Has he had a medical, or is he hanging around to see the doctor now? All the little signs.

In those last twenty-four, forty-eight hours, you end up in very close proximity to each other. It's the last place you want to be, sizing each other up across the room, bumping into each other in the lobby, sharing the lift on the way back up to your rooms. It's awkward, but the little tells are all there. If they're friendly, initiating conversation, trying to make jokes, it's obvious that they haven't got the heart for war. You know it long before you step into the ring.

You have to get him out of there early. The longer it goes on, the longer you let him survive, the worse it reflects on you. Try your man in the first thirty seconds, Emanuel always says. Get your first big punch in early, and try to knock him out. The opening seconds are the most dangerous. Your body hasn't acclimatised. It's not used to taking a punch. It hasn't taken a punch in weeks. You might be warm and loose and ready in the dressing room hitting pads, but you're not being hit yourself. A quick punch, a hard punch, it can hurt.

Pride makes a man dangerous. You're the visiting fighter in his hometown. His friends and family are there. When I fight James Cook in the Buffalo Run Casino, Miami, Oklahoma, his kids are in the front row of this tiny arena where they can see every punch that lands on their hero, and you can hear every word. *Hit him, Daddy. Hit him, Daddy.* He doesn't want to be embarrassed. He fights harder. I can't bring myself to punch this guy in the head in front of his little boys. I stop him with a body shot instead, a mercy kill.

‹ ›

I start to think I have it all. The great life, the unbeaten record, the Hall of Fame trainer, the big-money contract on the table.

Have it all except for the woman I love.

Maud won't answer my calls. When she does, she says she doesn't want to talk to me. She lives in New York now, moved there in summer 2007 with just her suitcase and her violin to chase her dream. We're closer geographically, but that's about it. We've been on again and off again since I moved to Detroit, and at the moment, we're definitely off. She's pretty clear in her reasons: I'm not the same Andy that she met and fell in love with. I've let America change me, either unable or unwilling to tell the difference between life in the real world and an ego massage from a sycophant. I can't see it. I don't even realise that it's happening but that's the trap of fame when you're caught up in the middle of it. Everyone else keeps telling me I'm great, and I can't understand why she doesn't feel the same. But as long as I keep carrying on like the man about town, she's not interested in knowing me.

I call in to see her at work one day during one of my trips to New York with Emanuel. She's behind the bar, not expecting me.

'Can we talk? I want to sort this out.'

'What's there to talk about? I've told you how I feel and nothing's changed.'

'Come on, let's just talk about it. Emanuel has invited us out for dinner at six. Come with me.'

Where it all started for me – the famous Repton Boxing Club in East London. The weights sessions got a little bit more difficult as I got older, unfortunately.

Starting out early at a gym show in Kent (that's me in the green and yellow Repton colours). When I saw Ned and Mushy boxing, I wanted to learn too, and I won two schoolboy titles in England before we moved to Limerick.

With Jesus Gonzales and Tony Davitt after I won silver at the World Junior Championships in 2002. Beating Gonzales turned out to be one of the biggest moments in my career, ultimately leading me to Detroit and to Emanuel. I was so exhausted that I don't remember any of the medal ceremony.

Devastation at the 2004 Olympics in Athens. In my heart, I knew that Hassan N'Dam had beaten me before the final result was even announced. My Olympic dream was over. (©MURAD SEZER/AP/Shutterstock)

I'll never forget my visit to Áras an Uachtaráin with the Irish Olympic team. It was a privilege to meet President Mary McAleese – and it was the first day I met Maud. (©INPHO/ Morgan Treacy)

You might not think it to look at, but through that red door is possibly the most famous boxing gym in the world: the Kronk. (©Tom Szczerbowski / Getty Images)

Emanuel always had his own way of doing things, whether it was wrapping hands or fixing cuts. This photo was taken before my first fight as a professional in March 2006, where I beat Anthony Cannon (*below*) on points to go 1-0. (*Top:* ©Bloomberg / Getty Images; *Bottom:* ©ASSOCIATED PRESS)

Emanuel trained more than 40 world champions over the course of his Hall of Fame career, including Tommy Hearns, Michael Moorer (pictured), Lennox Lewis, Wladimir Klitschko – and me. (©*The Ring Magazine* / Getty Images)

Doing padwork with Emanuel was one of the most intense workouts you can imagine. I don't think I ever managed more than four straight rounds. This photo was taken in the Belfast Kronk in 2007. (©INPHO/ PRESSEYE/Jonathan Porter)

I was always fortunate to have a great team in my corner. For my fight against Willie Gibbs, it was Emanuel (*left*), Joey Gamache (*second left*), and Sugar Hill (*right*). (©INPHO/James Crombie)

Emanuel's beautiful Rolls-Royce Corniche, freshly polished and gleaming. Little did we know …

Emanuel's house in Rosedale Park became my home as well, which meant myself and Sugar Hill never missed one of his famous backyard barbecues.

Emanuel was more than a coach to me, more than a mentor. He let me live my dream. (©INPHO/James Crombie)

Roger and I were pretty much inseparable when we were kids. We both know what the other is thinking without even needing to say a word most of the time, which made him an invaluable person to have in my corner throughout my career. (*Left:* ©INPHO/James Crombie)

Myself and Wladimir Klitschko got to know each other well through different training camps over the years. I learned a lot about being a champion by watching Wladimir and how he operated.

The greatest band you've never heard, The Klits – Michael Eaton, Wladimir Klitschko and me.

Meeting the Greatest, Muhammad Ali, at the re-opening of the legendary 5th Street Gym in Miami, Florida, in 2010.

Damian and I in Madison Square Garden for my fight against Dennis Sharpe in November 2006. Before I even turned pro, Damian was the main man taking care of business on my behalf outside the ring so that I could take care of it inside.

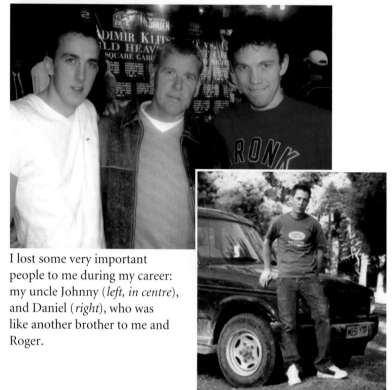

I lost some very important people to me during my career: my uncle Johnny (*left, in centre*), and Daniel (*right*), who was like another brother to me and Roger.

It took me and Adam a while to get used to working with each other, but once we did, we became close friends as well as fighter and coach. He transformed the way I fought, and I completely bought in to everything he told me. (*Top:* ©Dave Thompson / Stringer / Getty Images; *Bottom:* ©Tom Jenkins / Getty Images)

The night that I beat Matt Korobov and became WBO middleweight champion of the world, 13 December 2014. (*Top:* ©David Becker / Stringer / Getty Images; *Bottom:* ©INPHO/Raymond Spencer)

A dream come true. (©INPHO / Raymond Spencer)

My homecoming in Limerick after winning the world title was a night I'll never forget – but there was no harm getting a selfie, just in case. (©Diarmuid Greene / SPORTSFILE)

Maud and I in the summer of 2013. We've been on every step of this journey together from the start, through all of the ups and downs. I couldn't have done it without her.

My philosophy on boxing, borrowed from the film director Jim Jarmusch and painted on the walls of the National Stadium in Dublin. (©INPHO/James Crombie)

My final fight before retirement, against KeAndrae Leatherwood in Madison Square Garden, March 2017. (©INPHO/Tom Hogan)

On the short walk from the dressing room to the ring, you become a different man. You have to. (©Ramsey Cardy / Sportsfile / Getty Images)

We go for dinner that night, and then we spend the weekend together, talking, figuring things out. We still love each other. We'll make it work.

After the win against Daniels I have a few quick stoppages, which does absolutely nothing to keep my feet on the ground. Clinton Bonds lasts for about two minutes. Thomas Hengtsberger manages double that amount: he survives for four. HBO lists me as one of the five hottest prospects in the boxing world right now. *The Ring* magazine, the Bible of boxing, has me on their list too. People I barely know invite me to big parties in nice houses, just so that they can introduce me to their friends and say I'm there. I get presents sent to me in the mail, packages dropped off for me at the gym. The more I win, the more it happens, and I do nothing to discourage it. People start to treat me like a superstar. I start to believe it about myself.

Privately, Emanuel always set his expectations for me at the highest level from day one. You will be a world champion, Andy, and it won't take long. But he's much more measured when he's talking in public, walking the high-wire to perfection, pitching his comments right in the sweet spot between generating interest and the kind of theatrical, transparent hype that is quickly dismissed out of hand. Publicly, even when he's out there saying that he's excited as he was when he first laid eyes on Roy Jones Jr, he's careful to temper his comments: there's no rush; Andy's only learning his trade; it's far too early to be speaking about world titles. But it doesn't take long for things to accelerate. Once I get past Daniels, he's confident enough to go out there and tell reporters that I'll be a contender for a world title shot within a year.

The buzz spreads to Ireland. After a few quiet years, the country is falling in love with pro boxing again. Big nights in Dublin, sell-outs in the Point, Bernard Dunne building nicely towards his world title shot. I've been away for three years and now it's time to come home. It doesn't take much for Emanuel's positivity to start turning heads, filling column inches. Damian negotiates a deal for me with Brian Peters, the main promoter in Ireland: five fights, spread over the next couple of years, all to be shown live on RTÉ.

I keep ticking off the wins, home and away, one at a time. 12–0. 13–0. 14–0. I go back to Limerick in early 2008 to fight in my home city for the first time since my amateur days. When I stop Alejandro Falliga in the main event at UL, my record stands at fifteen fights, fifteen wins, twelve of those knockouts. We've packed a lot into my first two years as a pro.

Top Rank are interested in me again, and this time they're determined to get the deal done, no matter how complicated the chain of negotiation seems. I'm booked for a fight in March 2008 against Brian Vera in the Mohegan Sun. I don't know much about Uncasville, Connecticut, or about Vera for that matter. He'll fall like the others, and all of America will see this. My step up to the next level, my coming out party, will go out live on national television, ESPN's *Friday Night Fights*. I'll win this, sign with Top Rank, and after that, the sky's the limit. A HBO debut on Kelly Pavlik's undercard in June, most likely, and after that, I'll be right at the top of the list for a shot at Pavlik's title. He's the champion that Emanuel wants for me. Destroy is the word he uses when he's talking me up to reporters. Andy will destroy Kelly.

At the height of it all, I buy myself a car that's worthy of this new superstar lifestyle. A white BMW 7 Series, a 745li.

See it on a Sunday, buy it on a Wednesday; as obnoxious as it is impulsive. Emanuel loves it. By the time I get the car home, he already has his paint guy there to put the pinstripe along the side of it and put my name on the door handle, exactly the same as Emanuel's own cars. That's his thing. A white kid driving around Detroit in a white BMW 7 Series with his name on the side; I was looking for trouble. One night in the depths of winter, it very nearly found me.

I brace myself before I even open the door of the gym and step out onto the street. The cold stings. Detroit winter takes no prisoners. The temperature gauge in the car tells me it's minus six and I'd well believe it. I turn the engine on and the heating up.

I ring Maud and we're chatting away while I start to drive home, but then I get a notion and I spin the car around and head back in the other direction. Emanuel is out of town travelling for a few days, doing a HBO show, and Sugar Hill is gone to visit one of his former boxers in prison and I don't know what time he'll be back. I decide to pick up some food on the way home to save me cooking.

I pull into an empty parking lot outside this Mexican restaurant. It looks like Los Pollos Hermanos from *Breaking Bad* and almost certainly serves the kind of food I shouldn't be eating, and that's exactly what I'm in the mood for. I sit in the car, lights on, engine on, while I finish chatting to Maud. I'd never usually do that, and I'm familiar enough with this neighbourhood to know that it's not the kind of place that a guy like me in a car like this wants to hang around in for too long. Get in, get the food, get out. Ten minutes later, I'm still on the phone.

'OK, OK, I better go. I better get off the phone here before I get jacked.'

I'm laughing away to myself as we say goodbye, but as I put down the phone, a shadow moves in the rear-view mirror that catches my eye. There are two guys standing behind the car. I hadn't noticed anyone around when I pulled in to park. Now I see that there are two or three more guys on the other side of the car, standing around the dumpster, half-obscured. I've a funny feeling that this can only go one of two ways from here; either I get out of the car, or they'll find a way to remove me themselves.

I sit for a minute, and when I move, I try to do it in one smooth motion, as quickly as possible. Out, car door locked behind me, and make a beeline for the restaurant. As soon as I step out of the car, they start walking towards me. I pick up the pace, move a bit faster. The front door of the restaurant is only about ten yards away, thankfully, and I duck inside.

There's more adrenaline running through my body now than there was when I was doing my workout a half-hour ago. I try not to panic so I order some food, but it's going cold and I'm frantically trying to get Emanuel or Sugar Hill on the phone. Through the window I can see these guys, hoods up and heads down, hanging around the car.

I try Emanuel and Sugar Hill a few more times. Still no answer. I go through my phone but I don't have numbers for anyone else who might be able to come and help me. I sit there for half an hour, forty minutes, watching these guys watch my car. Emanuel calls me back eventually. I tell him the story.

'Emanuel, I think I'm going to be robbed here. Car jacked, like. I'm sitting inside the restaurant and these guys are just waiting out there for me to come out.'

'Alright, alright. You just wait there. I'll get someone to come help you.'

Five, maybe ten minutes later, this huge RV whips into the parking lot, like something straight out of *The A-Team* minus the theme tune, and pulls up outside the door of the restaurant. Four or five guys that I know from the Kronk jump out and start shouting. 'What's going on? What's going on?'

The driver, a guy called Ali Hakim, comes over to me. 'You OK? You OK, man? Where these guys at?'

Unsurprisingly, they're nowhere to be seen now. Ali's a big man, a former heavyweight fighter. Doing a runner was unquestionably their most sensible course of action. They've disappeared off into the night.

A boxer's style reflects his personality.

At my best in the ring, I'm measured, thoughtful, considered, strategic. But when it comes to it, when I'm challenged, I won't back down. Then you see me become stubborn, determined, headstrong, even borderline reckless at times. Never question my heart for the fight. I won't back down, I won't shy away. If you want to go to war, let's go to war. Let's have it.

Everyone can appreciate a slugfest, a barnburner, two guys giving it their all and going at it hell for leather for twelve rounds, or however long it lasts until one of them drops. It's treated us to some of the best fights in boxing history. But there's real beauty, artistry, in watching two great technical boxers trying to out-think each other. The million little calculations that each one of them is making, and the amount of mental energy that it takes up. Thinking two or three steps ahead, trying to figure out how you can manoeuvre your opponent into position, not through power or brute force, but by convincing him that is the position that he actually wants to be in, needs to be in. Leading him towards the trap before he is even aware that one has been set. You need to train his brain, feed it visual cues in the way you move your arms, your legs, your head. Allow it to detect a pattern – but always the pattern that you want him to see. Slowly, carefully. If you move too fast, if you rush things, he'll spot your game and all of that work, all of that planning, will be for nothing. That's where the art comes – in doing that, maintaining that level of concentration, that focus, and then drawing on the same amount of mental energy again, if not more, to make sure that you don't fall into his trap, that the hunter doesn't become the hunted.

In a fight, your two minds work in harmony, your conscious mind and your subconscious. All of your training is sharpened through repetition – the techniques, the pad-work, the drills – so that when you step out of the gym and into the ring, you do it without even thinking. In the heat of battle, it becomes instinctive. That is your subconscious mind. Your conscious mind is the mind that reads the fight as it unfolds, deciphers that information, and uses it. You see things and you react. Every time I jab him, he jabs me right back. Next time, I'll feint the jab, fool him, and when he goes to jab me back, I'll step outside and counter him.

When they complement each other, that is where the beauty comes. He throws a jab, and I slip it and throw a left hand at the same time. I step away and think, that's the shot I want from now on. It's a great punch, but I had it done before I even made the decision.

The circumstances of the fight often dictate which mind takes precedence. Early in your career, when guys are not on your level, you have to find a way to break them down. You have to be methodical and analytical. But when a fight is fought at a higher intensity, when it's more closely contested, it's a more instinctive thing. The subconscious mind takes over. The autopilot kicks in.

Emanuel teaches me how to play poker. I've never played before but different people call over to the house in the evenings for a game, casual, fun, and I learn. I've a similar style at the poker table as I do in the ring: measured, doing the calculations, trying to out-think everyone else. And then there are the moments when all of that cautious logic goes out the window. These are the cards I have, this is the hand I have to play. I go for it, even if I know the odds are stacked against me.

It hurts you when you lose a hand. I play a lot of chess against Roger, and it hurts when you lose a big piece. It hurts when you get caught with a good shot in the ring. But no matter what game you're playing, the only thing to do is accept it, recover, and find a way to rebuild from the position you're in.

Sometimes, though, you just want to react.

*I*t is time for our main event. Mohegan Sun Arena has long been the place where unbeaten prospects launch their career to the next level. Tonight against Brian Vera, Andy Lee trying to take off to stardom. Many feel it's his destiny. Four days removed from St Patrick's Day, Lee ready to show southern New England that the luck of the Irish has blessed him with the skill and the will. It's a path he's been travelling on since his childhood on the banks of the River Shannon ...

Luke knocks on the door of my room. Maud's downstairs in the lobby. She's just arrived in. We don't usually see each other on the day of a fight. That's the routine we've developed. We'll talk on the phone, I'll say whatever I can to try to reassure her, tell her I love her, that it will all be fine, that I'll see her later. I think it makes it easier for both of us, helps take a lot of the emotion out of the day. I'm not worrying about how she's feeling, and she's not seeing me and getting nervous. A bit of superstition as well, so that's just the way that we do things. But I want to see her now. I'm ready for this guy, and seeing my girlfriend isn't going to undo that. I ask Luke to go down to her, tell her where I am, get her to come up to see me. She'll say no, but convince her. Tell her it's fine, I'm fine, totally chilled out.

I think Vera is trying to throw Lee off a bit, do something you don't expect him to do, box a little bit, but sooner or later, Vera is going to do what he does, which is come in that front door... Lee just hurt him there with that left hand, and Brian Vera goes down!

145

I bounce off the bed when I hear her knock, swing open the door, and pull her close to me. We hang out for forty-five minutes, maybe an hour, the two of us lying on top of the bed, chatting, half-watching TV. I give her the little present that I've brought for her. She loves it, surprised that I had the time to go pick a present out when I'm getting ready for a fight. You look great, she tells me, so relaxed, so confident. Much bigger than usual on fight day. Don't be worrying, I tell her, I'm gonna put on a show. This guy is gonna be out of there in a couple of minutes. We're gonna have a great night. We go back to watching the TV.

The problem for Vera, as he comes in, he leaves holes, he leaves gaps, and those gaps are being filled by the counterpunch of Lee. Styles make fights but the style of Lee makes him the fighter that he is. It's very difficult to deal with a southpaw who's this tall and knows how to stay tall ... Vera hurt him – let me tell you, Lee is hurt for the first time in his pro career! That right hand can be successful against southpaws. That hurt Lee.

I might look big but I'm not. Vera came in bang on the contract weight at 162lbs at the weigh-in yesterday but I didn't even make it to 159lbs. It's the lightest I've ever been for a fight. Not by design; by accident. By carelessness. We didn't bring scales with us, and the ones we bought in the shop when we got here were different to the ones we usually use. We thought we had them calibrated properly, but we didn't. I didn't realise until I stood up for my official weight. I was in the sauna yesterday morning, shedding weight that I didn't even need to lose. Part of the routine. Sugar Hill and Aaron were there too. Aaron was coming in heavy for his own fight tonight so the two of us stayed in there with him to help him. I should have just got out, realised when enough was enough. That's easy to say now in hindsight. I try to rehydrate as best I can, take on as much fluid as possible, but my body doesn't want it. Now I'm giving Vera all of this weight, a big advantage. I don't say it to anyone, but there's a sliver of doubt there.

Lee was in control of things until the closing moments of round two when some confidence came Vera's way. He's got a clubbing right hand that landed, and he hurt Lee … When Vera did hurt Lee in the last round with that right hand it was because he was able to get in close. Again, not that Lee is Superman, but if he had a kryptonite, that kryptonite would be when guys get in close. In-fighting is not something that Lee is comfortable with … Both men landing well at the end of this third round. It's turning into an entertaining fight between Vera and Lee.

Emanuel's been funny the last few days too. Much quieter than usual. A bit on edge. I think he's noticed something, picked up on a vibe or an emotion, something intangible, the way Emanuel usually does. Whatever it is, whatever he's concerned about, he keeps it to himself. He's not going to trouble me with intangibles now.

Look at Vera work on the inside, digging in, opening up a cut. There's a cut that's opened up! A gash across the top of the right eye of Andy Lee. Big action round here … Lee walking forward with his hands down and lands a left hand. Vera says, 'Bring it, you're going to get it back!' Right now, Vera eating those left hands from Lee.

We clash heads and a cut opens up over my eye, but other than that I'm winning, just like everyone expected. Winning easily. My power shots are landing, juddering, and when he comes back, I've got more for him. But he's a tough, tough man. He might not be able to beat me but he's not going to stand there and let me walk through him, like so many of the others have. He's not going to disgrace himself like that. He keeps coming back, quicker every time, putting his body on the line, and somehow he's the one dictating, not me. Maud screams at me but I can't hear her: use your jab, use your jab. I need to be smart. Disengage. Bring him for a walk around the ring. Feint. Tie him up. But my inexperience betrays me. He's pressing me, pressing me, and the only thing I can do is punch. It's too fast. I'm not in control.

A very active finish to that fourth round, highly entertaining, as Brian Vera is hanging in there tough with Andy Lee after being knocked down in the opening round by a left hand, a 10–8 opening round for Lee … He's just digging down and trying to make a fight of it is Brian Vera, and backing up Lee, as Lee picks his spots and tries to catch Vera coming in.

There's no let up at all in the pace. He's still coming at me, still coming at me, and when he hits me, he hurts me. You've got this fight, Emanuel tells me, just a few more rounds, keep boxing, keep moving your legs. I can't. My legs are completely shot. They're gone. I can't move them. And I see it so many times in fights over the years: if one fighter gets on top early and doesn't capitalise on his advantage, can't hammer it home and lets the other guy hang around, that guy who should have been out of there long, long ago will come back to win and break his heart.

First three rounds, Brian Vera had forty-six connects. In the last two rounds alone, he's had sixty-eight connects and opened up a cut over the right eye of the hot prospect Andy Lee, and swarming him to open up this sixth round. Lots of pressure we've seen recently from Vera … Vera knows obviously that there's a cut over that right eye of Lee, and Vera not being careful with his head on the inside, being a bit of a billy-goat, letting his head swing around a little bit … Teddy's scorecard is 49–45 to Lee. He had a 10–8 round to open things up but Vera has made a fight of it here in these middle rounds.

I ring my mam and my dad after every fight if they're not there. It could be all hours of the night back home in Ireland. It doesn't matter. A quick chat just to hear my mam's voice: hi, Mam, it's me, I won. You can go back to sleep now, I'll tell you about it properly in the morning. Night.

The phone doesn't ring tonight. When it finally does, it's Roger who wakes my mam up, not me.

Back and forth they go, Vera trying to chase Lee across the ring. Right hand comes in. Blood streaming down the right side of his face. It was his world when he entered the ring, unbeaten and pretty. Ain't pretty no more. It was said before, it's coming true tonight. Brian Vera looking for the upset … OH! Big shot ends it. What an upset! Brian Vera has done it. Andy Lee is no longer unbeaten. Quick stoppage. He was battered, bruised, bloodied, and now he is no longer unbeaten.

It's late by the time I get back to the hotel, long after midnight. Maud and Roger have been crying. The stitches over my right eye are still fresh, the reds and purples on my face still vibrant. My lip is swollen from where my tooth punctured a hole in it and came through the other side. I put on a brave face and tell them I'm fine, that the doctors checked me over in the hospital, that it's only bumps and bruises. We should go to sleep.

For days the thought of sleep is a delusion. Instead I lie there and relive it all from more angles than the cameras could ever hope to capture. Vera's putting it on me, putting it on me, his right like a cannon, but I'm still moving. I'm still there. The referee breaks us, looks at me, and asks me if I'm OK. I am. I nod. We carry on, into the centre of the ring, and I fight back. I let my hands drop and somehow find the power in my legs to swing the right hook that will finally shake Vera off. He ducks underneath it and counters with another lethal right hand of his own. Devastating power, but my arms carry on with their combo in spite of it, like a reflex. I have a hard left already dialled in and I knock him backwards, stagger him. But now the referee is pushing him off me, separating us, and shepherding me back to my corner. It can't be over. I landed the punch. I landed the last punch. I want to fight on but I'm being forced on to a stool. I have to answer the doctor's stupid questions, tell him where I am, who I am. I want to fight on. It's over, Andy. It's over.

I wonder if it will ever be over, or if I'll have to live forever with this shame I'm feeling.

I add more and more detail to the scene as the days go by, every conversation presenting a fresh opportunity to torment myself in glorious technicolour. The ecstasy of Vera's family and friends as they celebrate: *I fuckin told yalls he'd do it, I fuckin told yalls*. Maud was there to hear it, stunned in place beside them, and now I am too. I can see her sitting in the empty toilet cubicle, unable to face the sympathetic small talk of strangers, and then alone in the silence of the empty arena until Luke came to find her, to tell her that I was fine but had been taken to hospital as a precaution. I picture Roger as he opens the door of our room to her, the whites of his eyes streaked red. Roger never cries. She's sitting in the bathroom again when I call, letting one hour melt into the next until the doctors let me go and I come back and tell her that it will all be OK.

I don't know that it will. Sitting in the hospital beside me, Emanuel doesn't sugarcoat it.

'You were winning the fight. You had him down. And then you fought the wrong fight. That was a big fight. You know it's going to be hard to come back from this.'

He's hurting too. He tells me about the night that Tommy Hearns lost against Sugar Ray Leonard.

'I stayed up all night crying that night. It was worse for me than it was for Tommy.'

The limo that we hired for after the fight, a little treat to mark a huge night in my career, sits there untouched. The driver takes us all back to Maud's apartment in New York the next day, barely a word said by anyone. The wounds are fresh enough without the salt. I keep it together for another day, gloss over any attempts to console me and find refuge in the same vague reassurances. It will be OK. We drop Roger down to the bus station in Port Authority the following day so that he can head to the airport and catch his flight back to Limerick. We don't ever hug, but now I give him one because it's easier than trying to find the words to apologise. I've let him down too.

Luke asks me how I'd feel about doing an interview on camera. I flick through the pages of an old magazine, roll the lens cover of one of his cameras through my hands, anything to occupy my mind. I examine every decision, relive every mistake. I think about what Emanuel said, how I'd fought the wrong fight. There's two sides to everyone once they step into the ring – the boxer and the fighter, the conscious and the subconscious. I let Vera goad me into engaging the wrong one at the wrong time. I saw his toughness in the face of my early dominance as an affront, felt that it somehow made him more of a man than me. When he drew me in to stand and trade, I should have stuck to my strengths and let him box himself out, frustrate himself with wild swipes at my shadow. Instead, I bit, and it has cost me everything.

My unbeaten record is gone. The Top Rank deal is definitely gone; they won't want anything to do with a loser. The plans to have another homecoming fight in Ireland next month will have to be shelved while I let my injuries heal. There'll be no HBO fight in June, no stepping-stone to a world title fight. That bullish talk about a shot at Pavlik later in the year, taking his belt, it seems so spectacularly misguided in hindsight that maybe it's for the best that that's gone too. All of the doubters, everyone who said that I was just an Emanuel Steward hype job, I can see the smirks of vindication. I can't even offer a response.

I go back to a Detroit for a day or two and pack a bag. I can't go home to Limerick right now. I want to be in New York with Maud, in a big impersonal city, some place where I can disappear into the crowd and be anonymous. Maud, my family, my friends, they can see how badly it is eating me up. I can't hide it from them, but they're experiencing this for the first time too. When every fight is built up as life and death, eventually you start to believe it, and we don't have the experience or the perspective to confidently say that it will all be OK in the end. One of my friends, Darryl Doyle, reassures me, tells me that it's just a bump in the road; it's the first time I've ever heard that phrase.

When I get back to training and back to Detroit, the hangers-on are nowhere to be seen. The world where you're the blue-eyed boy and everyone wants to be with you and shake your hand and high-five you, oh yeah, you the man, Andy, you the man – that all changes. It's the most valuable lesson that I learn from the whole experience: the buzz and the backslaps and the *ya boyas*, take it all with a pinch of salt, especially when things are going well. And when the crowd clears, only the people who really matter will still be there.

A little kid comes up to me in the gym. I know him. He can't be older than eight or nine. He's always there with his dad and his brothers; there must be five or six of them, all boxers. We're always messing around and joking, and I can tell he looks up to me. He sees me come in the door, and before I even have the bag off my shoulder, he comes over to me.

'What happened in that fight, man? What did you do? What did you do?'

'Ah, you know, I lost.'

I need to give him a bit more than that.

'Yeah, but why did you lose?'

'I didn't train hard enough and I underestimated him.'

He tries to give me a little pep talk and I'm really very grateful. I appreciate how much he cares. He was inconsolable on the night of the fight, his dad tells me. He was allowed to stay up late to watch it live and started crying when I was beaten.

We fly out to the Austrian Alps for another training camp with Wladimir and his team. It's good to get away and immerse myself in hard work, but all of the doubts still linger. I look at Wladimir, three defeats on his record and still world heavyweight champion. He's been through it all before.

'How did you deal with your first loss?'

A couple of weeks out from a fight is not the time to be asking about old defeats. He doesn't really want to go there, drag up bad memories and relive them, but he humours me.

'Look, Andy, you just have to get back in there and do it. That's all you can do.'

I want to mine him for every bit of information he has: how he felt in the days and weeks afterwards, his thought process, a checklist of things to do, his roadmap back to the top. But I leave it at that.

From the moment the referee stepped between me and Vera, all I want to do is get back into the ring and fight. That's the only way to right the wrong. I have to wait four months to do it, and when the time comes, I want it to send out a message. Brian Peters books Willie Gibbs to face me in the University of Limerick in July 2009. He's Bernard Hopkins's cousin, from Philadelphia: a real fighter, 20–3. Willie Gibbs never fought Brian Vera, but if he did, he'd beat him all day, every day. I'm not coming back in at the same level again. I'm taking a step up to prove that Vera, as Darryl says, was just a bump in the road.

This time it has to be different. I coasted into the Vera fight. I didn't make any real changes to my training, despite the fact that the fight was scheduled for ten rounds and I had never gone more than six before that night. I was foolish enough to think that I could make that step up without any sort of extra conditioning if the fight went into the late rounds, and complacent enough to think that it would never last that long anyway. Losing to Vera might have been the making of me, because if I'd carried on with that kind of attitude, it would have only been a matter of time before I got a worse beating.

Sugar Hill becomes more and more involved in my training, and he takes the lead for this camp. When people first meet him, they never know how to take him because he's such a unique character, and I didn't know how to take him either. For one thing, he doesn't like it when people call him Javan – Sugar was what his grandmother called him, so Sugar it is. We got to know each other a little bit in those first few years. He was still working as a Detroit police officer when I first moved out to live here, and I always felt safe when he was around. We would play cards, play pool, go bowling on a Tuesday night, but up until the Vera fight, I think he saw me as just another kid on the Kronk conveyor belt: he expected me to stick around for a while and then fade away and head home. The Vera fight hurt him as much as it hurt anyone. After that, he could see that me and Roger were genuine, honest, hard workers, that we weren't just there for the ride or to take advantage of Emanuel's generosity.

When your confidence is at rock bottom, you'll reach out for anyone to embrace you. I want someone who will work with me and push me on, and after I lose, Emanuel seems a little bit disinterested. Sugar Hill puts his faith in me, as well as his time and his energy, and I respond. Over the years we become very close friends as well as coach and boxer. We go out every weekend when I'm not fighting or in camp. He's someone who cares deeply for me, Roger, Maud, my family, someone who always stays in touch. If anything was ever to go wrong, he's one of the people I know would have my back.

When we start working together for the Gibbs fight, I train harder than I have ever done before and he's the one pushing me through it. He makes little tweaks to my style, definitely changes it for the better. He has picked up a lot of insights from Emanuel over the years in terms of attitude and mindset, but technically he does things differently. Emanuel is more about fighting off rhythm, whereas Sugar Hill is more methodical and more focused on how to impose yourself on your opponent. He teaches me a lot of the elements that I was missing against Vera when I needed them the most: how to fight on the inside, where to put your head and where not to, being strong, holding your man, tying him up and dominating him. A week before I face Gibbs, I open my laptop, and for the one and only time in my life, I load up a clip from the Vera fight. Just the last twenty seconds. I watch it, relive it, and then close it. I've trained ten times harder, ticked every box in my preparation. The clip is the final 1 per cent.

Gibbs is a showman. I hardly see him wearing a shirt from the moment he arrives until the moment he leaves. He shows up and means business, in immaculate shape, and he wants everyone in Limerick city to see it, not just me. At the press conference, he talks the talk:

'I'm still scratching my head about this fight. The guy just suffered his first defeat and they want him to suffer a second one.'

All the pressure is on me, and he's happy to turn it up and see if I crack. I lie in bed and I imagine how he punches, how he throws his jab, what I'll do when he throws his jab, how I can punch against him. It's insecurity, and it's constantly on my mind. I wonder how he's training. I open the laptop again and start searching for clues. Who is his coach? Where is his gym? Who is he sparring with? What do I think of those guys? All the time, I'm trying to pick up any insight, anything that I can latch on to for confidence, no matter how small.

Driving to the arena, the thought crosses my mind: this could be it. This could be the last time I ever drive this route as a professional boxer. Because if I lose tonight, that's surely the end for me. It's the last worried thought I have because, as soon as I get into the dressing room, it's everything it should be – relaxed, playful, fun – and I know that there's no way I'm losing this fight. Roger turns up the music and we have a dance-off. We're singing and we're laughing, and people are drifting in and out of the dressing room, giving us instructions, doing their checks, wondering if we've lost the plot completely.

When I get into the ring, I look straight at Willie Gibbs for the first time all week. Up until that point, looking at him meant catching a glimpse of him out of the corner of my eye at the press conferences and at the weigh-in and getting worked up that this guy looks like he's in good shape, he's got a good team here with him, he's focused. But now I look into his eyes and I see nothing. And I think, I'm going to fucking knock you out.

I do. I stop him in the last round; his corner throw in the towel with five seconds left.

The next morning, my mam cooks a big breakfast in the house. It's a tradition we have, the last chance for everyone to say goodbye before we scatter to the four corners again. There's usually a good bit of fight talk and it makes me a bit uncomfortable, sitting there listening to people praise me. I'd brush it off and try to change the subject. Ah yeah, go on, that's it now, it's done. But this time I let them talk away and don't try to stop it. I sit there and listen and soak it up and enjoy it. Now that I know what it feels like to lose, I won't ever take this feeling for granted again.

I drop Emanuel and the others off at the airport and on the way back home, for the first time in months, I allow myself a genuine smile. And I think to myself, I'm back.

〈 〉

In the moments before you leave the dressing room – on the walk from the dressing room through the back area of the arena, in the tunnel, and on the walk through the crowd to the apron – in those moments, you're changing, you become somebody else. You leave behind your usual self, the man that you are outside the ring, and become the fighter. You have to allow yourself to forget all of your best, most compassionate instincts. Abandon yourself to the transformation and be this entirely different person. Nasty. Spiteful. Brutal.

That's professional fighting's unwritten agreement. When we sign the contract, when we shake hands at the press conference, we both understand that I'm going to try to hurt you and you're going to try to hurt me, and we're both OK with that. I don't hate you. I probably don't even dislike you. But I'm there and this is my job. It's your job, too. I accept that. I don't feel bad that you're going to try to hurt me. I don't take offence to the fact that you will do whatever it takes. I expect nothing less. In amateur boxing, hurting your opponent is not part of the ethos. It's not the goal. It's about outmanoeuvring your opponent, hitting without being hit, scoring points. But in the pros, you have to embrace that viciousness. You never go in thinking, I'm going to damage this guy and it's going to be permanent, but you have to fully want to hurt your opponent, to knock him out, because that's what you have to do to win the fight. Most boxers take this approach, share that same understanding. And once the fight is over, straight after the bell, the first thing they'll do is meet in the middle and share a hug of mutual respect and admiration, because it's nothing personal. It's just the game.

I don't regret anything I've ever done in the ring – no pain I've ever inflicted, no punch I've thrown that I wish I could take back. There are times, maybe, when I have been cruel. Jason McKay and his coach, John Breen, questioned my heart in the build-up to our fight in Dublin in 2007. The tin man, they called me. All tin, no heart. It was a tactic, the only thing they could do to try to get under my skin and put me off. I brushed it off in the press conferences but I let it get to me; it hurt me, and I purposely punished McKay for it in the ring. I could have stopped him early on but I drew it out instead. I never tried to knock him out, I never tried to go for the kill. It was poetic in the end because it was their hearts that were tested, not mine: Breen's heart as a coach, his compassion. Did he feel for his fighter who was clearly being dominated? And McKay's heart as a fighter. Did he want to continue, did he want to keep fighting when he was taking such punishment? He didn't come back out at the end of the sixth round; Breen wouldn't let him, and McKay had no complaints.

In boxing, you're only ever one or two losses away from becoming yesterday's story, from the end of your career. Your life, your living, is on the line. Your prospects, your opportunities, they all hinge on the outcome, all depend on you winning. When you're in a fight, you are effectively making huge life decisions every second, with every punch you throw, with every move you make. If you're working in a normal job and you make a big decision that will affect your future, you discuss it with your family. You might ask your friends for their advice. You consider the impact that the decision will have on you and everyone else, the pros and the cons, and you weigh it all up. But when you're in the ring, you're making those decisions on the fly, a thousand times over in every fight. One head movement, one punch, a moment too early or a moment too late, can change the course of your life.

Physical pain is nothing. It isn't. You don't get hurt in fights. You rarely feel the shots land, even the heavy ones. Physiologically, the pain is transmitted from the source to your brain, but there's no time to think about it, no time to even acknowledge it. Your brain is in a constant sensory overload with the sights and sounds and smells of combat, adrenaline coursing through your body like a fuel, and the messages that those pain receptors are trying to deliver are insignificant at best. They get pushed to the back of the queue. They can be dealt with later. It's a battle phenomenon. In sparring, you feel the impact of shots a lot more because there's not the same intensity to the fight, the same urgency to get on with things. Or in the corner between rounds, when the cutman squeezes the top of your eyebrow to clean out the deepening gash and stitch it back together again, it stings for a moment. But as soon as the bell goes, you're out there again and the thought of the cut fades to irrelevance.

When you get a black eye and go into school or are walking down the street and people say, 'Oh what happened? You must have lost your fight,' it always perplexes me. It's just a black eye, I think to myself. I wear them like they're nothing. It's no big deal. It just happens in the ring. It's not an indicator of how well or how badly you're fighting. I'm fortunate: I've a couple of scars on my face, a few damaged teeth, and a bit of discomfort when I hold my hands in a certain position. All very minor stuff, and that's it. The bumps and the cuts and the bruises, they come with the territory. It's an occupational hazard, part and parcel of the job that you've signed up for.

But the emotional pain is something that you can never prepare for or get used to or get over. The night I lost to Vera was one of the only times I've ever had to go to hospital after a fight. Whatever physical pain I was feeling as I sat there and the doctors checked me over was totally insignificant, absolutely nothing compared to the torture that was eating me up from the inside out. It picked apart my confidence, crippled my self-esteem. You get over things in time, but it takes a lot of time. I see fighters who can lose a fight and brush it off like it means nothing to them. I don't know if I admire them or if I think they're idiots. It's almost ignorant, and it makes me wonder if fighting, winning, ever meant that much to them in the first place. Maybe they're in it for the wrong reasons, maybe they don't have that expectation to be the best. But that was always my expectation.

Memory should be a teacher, not a torment. It should remind you of the mistakes that you've made so that you learn from them. Your past actions should inform your future ones, so that the next time you're faced with a similar choice, you don't make the same mistakes over and over again. That's how it should be. But it's human nature that when you make a bad decision, it won't leave you alone. The whys and the what ifs are never out of your mind. The negativity interrupts the most mundane moments of your day just to remind you that it's still there. It steals into that place of peace at night between closing your eyes and falling asleep. It haunts you into restlessness.

‹ ›

I sit in the reception area of Dr Pearlman Hicks's clinic and wait to be called. I felt the cut on my right eye re-open the second that Gibbs caught me. It was never going to take much to set it off again but he came in hard anyway, head-to-head. We were able to do enough to close it up until the end of the fight. It was my own fault for leaving my head there in the first place.

I sit there and I can't help but think: why is this being done now? The time to get this sorted was a year and a half ago, before I started collecting an album full of photos that look like I've just had a rough day at the abattoir. The same cut has been there since before the Vera fight, red, raw, a bullseye for my opponents' target practice. The tissue was tender to the touch. It was obvious, so obvious that people were asking me in the weeks beforehand if I'd be OK to fight. Asking out of concern, not out of curiosity. If people on the street were noticing it, it's a safe bet that the man who was trying to knock me out probably would too.

And I went ahead and fought anyway. Vera loved leaving the head in – real scrappy, dirty tactics. That's not why he beat me, but of all the things that are still annoying me about that night, the cut is top of the list. Emanuel is the most experienced trainer in the world. If there was any doubt about my eye, and to look at it, there clearly was, he should have pulled the fight. I might have protested but I would have listened. A little break to let it heal up properly would have done me no harm. I would have been ready to fight again by the summer. Instead, we rushed in, tried to keep that momentum snowballing. Andy Lee wins again. Andy Lee wins again.

I'm not angry with Emanuel because of the cut. I'm angry with Emanuel because the cut represents everything that went wrong in the build-up to the Vera fight. We didn't take the little things seriously at all in our preparations, and Emanuel was as responsible for that as anyone. He was doing a great job of promoting me and getting my name out there, telling everybody that I'd kick ass and presuming I would, but the nitty gritty of the work wasn't being done. This anger, it's not a coping mechanism. It's not something that I've fashioned out of the bitterness of defeat. When we got to fight night and I could sense that he was a bit worried, it annoyed me then. There's no point in you being worried now, I thought to myself. The time for that has passed.

This guy, Dr Hicks, is the best in the business. When Vitali Klitschko needed sixty stitches to put his face back together after Lennox Lewis went to town on it, Pearlman Hicks was the man he called to do the job. He cuts around the scar tissue on my right eye: the track lines left by cuts and stitches and cuts and stitches done hurriedly in the corner between rounds. The cutman has less than a minute to get you fixed up and ready to fight again. They don't have time to fully clean out a cut. They just stitch you right up, and all of the dirt is left under the skin in hard lumps and bumps. It's easy for an opponent to open it back up again; all it takes is one well-placed shot. After I get this procedure done, Emanuel never lets a ringside doctor stitch me up again. The next time I get cut, against Alexander Sipos, he takes me back to the dressing room and puts peroxide right in the cut. It bubbles up and cleans the wound out completely, drawing out all of this green pus and dirt and cocoa butter and Vaseline, and then he takes out a little needle and stitches me up himself. I never get badly cut again.

Doctor Hicks finishes the job and sends me on my way.

'Leave those stitches in for a week until it's all healed up, and then go get them taken out.'

I do exactly as he tells me, wait a week and then go to the plastic surgeon in Detroit that he has recommended. He takes the stitches out and puts the Steri-Strips on, but he's not entirely happy.

'You'll need to be careful. It still looks very tender.'

When I wake the next day, whatever way I've slept on it, the cut is open again. By eleven o'clock, I'm back on a plane to California, back to Dr Hicks's office to get the procedure redone. It's eight months before I'm able to get back in the ring and fight again.

With no way to build on it, the win against Gibbs starts to feel like a false dawn. I'm in the gym every day, but I can't get Emanuel's attention at all. At home, it's like nothing has changed. We're as close as ever. But he becomes less and less involved in my training until, by the end of the year, he's barely working with me. The doubts come easily. I wonder if he's lost faith in me and that's why he's not taking as much of an interest. If he saw something against Vera or since then that has made him realise that he got me all wrong, that I'll never be good enough to be a world champion. Sugar Hill effectively takes over as my head trainer. Joey Gamache, the former world lightweight champion, is working out of the Kronk now as an assistant coach to Emanuel and he becomes a lot more involved as well.

I make my comeback in Dublin the night Bernard Dunne stops Ricardo Cordoba and wins the world title, March 21st 2009. The Irish rugby team win the Six Nations that afternoon, the country's first Grand Slam since 1948. The O2 is absolutely electric and I'm just happy to be back home, back in the ring, and back winning again. Emanuel does the pre-fight media. He's there in my corner on fight night. But none of that is any use to me if I don't have his undivided attention in the gym. I can't accept that he has all of his other commitments – his other fighters, his HBO job, a life and a family of his own. Sugar Hill is a top coach, a great friend, and we develop an excellent understanding of each other, but I didn't turn pro to be trained by Sugar Hill; I turned pro to be trained by Emanuel.

Damian calls occasionally to check in and see how I'm getting on.

'Are you getting any time with Emanuel this week?'

The answer is always no. The frustration, the anger, builds and builds but I don't say it. I'm afraid to, afraid it might damage our relationship. Instead I keep going to the gym and hope that everything will eventually go back to normal.

I finally crack when we go to Vegas in May for the Ricky Hatton–Manny Pacquiao fight. I break down in the back of the limo, and all of the hurt and worry comes out in a torrent.

'What's going on? You're never around, I'm in Detroit by myself the whole time, and my career's all over the place. What am I doing here?'

There's not much Emanuel can say to make me feel better.

'You're right. I have to agree with you.'

And nothing changes. I'm offered a slot on Wladimir's next show in Gelsenkirchen. When I was winning, every fight was part of a plan. The dates, the opponents, they all fit together to make up the bigger picture, signposts marking out the road to the top. Now I'm stumbling around blindly from undercard to undercard without as much as a compass, never mind a map. I'll take that fight in Germany because I've no other option. I can't go on like this. I need to get out. It's not part of any long-term strategy, but I'm worried that if I stay, I'll become so resentful that I'll say or do something that I'll regret. So I don't say a word to anyone; I just pack my bags, head to New York to visit Maud for a few days, and I don't come back. We get an apartment together.

I don't speak to Emanuel for months, for the entire time that I'm living there. It's too hurtful to talk. I used to feel that we were always on the same page, that we understood each other's thoughts and emotions, a kind of telepathy. Now I'm not sure if that was ever true. My phone doesn't ring, and I don't feel the need to pick it up and call him. Anything that we'd say to each other would only make things worse.

I've already been booked for two more fights in Limerick and the first, in November against a decent French fighter, Affif Belghecham, is rapidly approaching. Joey Gamache lives in New York. He's somebody I know, somebody that I'm used to working with, and it seems like a natural move to go and train with him.

'I'm staying here, I'm not going back to Detroit. Will you train me? Can you find us a gym somewhere that we can use?'

'Yeah, of course.'

He knows I'm in a tough situation, that all is not right between me and Emanuel. I'm sure Emanuel doesn't appreciate him getting involved, and it affects their relationship too, but he wants to help me out. If anyone asks about

Emanuel, we don't say a word. Joey is stepping in to cover temporarily while he's away with his TV commitments. That's the official line.

There's real New York grit in some of the places that Joey takes me to, properly rough gyms in the Bronx. He seems to know his way around so I trust him. He must have a phone-book full of hard-hitting southpaws because everyone who gets in to spar with me is ready for the challenge. We work on my movement and angles, how to slip Belghecham's attacks, move my head, catch him by surprise, get him turned. It's different to how I'm used to fighting. I'm so invested in the Kronk style that I don't fully take Joey's instructions on board or appreciate them. It's only much later in my career that I master these skills and I come to understand the importance of what he was trying to teach me.

It's my mam who tells me about the letters first.

'Andy, why are we getting post here for you?'

'I dunno, Mam. Open it there, see what it is.'

'It looks important. From the lawyers. Something about the fight.'

Perry, the investors in Chicago, they're spooked by the whole thing after Vera. Overnight, their pocket aces are starting to look a bit more like 7–2 off suit. They have been pumping all of this money into my career, my development, hundreds of thousands of dollars, but when it comes to the crunch, they've no legal standing with me at all. The only contract I have is my management agreement with Emanuel.

I fly to Chicago with Emanuel in May 2008, a couple of weeks after the Vera fight, for a meeting with the investors to resolve everything. Damian dials in on a conference call. It's agreed to restructure my management contract, making it clear that Emanuel is the boxing manager but formally including the investment group by giving Perry the title of business manager. I hope that's everything sorted, but it drags on and on. We're all committed to working things out, to working together, but a year and a half later, the paperwork still hasn't been signed. Now they're sending send cease and desist letters to the house in Limerick and to Brian Peters, insisting that they are my managers and that I've gone rogue by relocating to New York. They haven't agreed for me to fight against Belghecham, and if it goes ahead, we'll all be sued.

I tell my mam not to bother with the letters, that I'll take care of them, and I get back to preparing for the fight. I'm so frustrated at this point that the best thing seems to be to just blow everything up – my involvement with them, my relationship with Emanuel – and start again from scratch. I know I've done nothing wrong, and I'm not going to see a fight cancelled because of a scare tactic. I can't see what the problem is. Everyone has been getting exactly what they're owed from these Irish purses; I'm taking my cut, and I'm sending Emanuel his share and their share of the rest as agreed. I go ahead and fight Belghecham anyway and beat him comfortably on points.

I'm supposed to be concentrating on my boxing, finding a way to get my career back on track. Instead, I'm living in New York, I'm not speaking to Emanuel, and I'm getting legal letters to try and stop me from fighting. It's non-stop phone calls and emails and the stress and uncertainty is overwhelming. Damian gets me some lawyers of my own, two of the best attorneys in New York, Keith Sullivan and David Berlin, and they arrange for a mediation meeting in Chicago to try and resolve everything after the Belghecham fight.

I spend days in our apartment searching through old emails and text messages, printing off the ones I need to bring with me, filling the new briefcase that Maud has just bought me. In twenty-five years, I've never needed a briefcase. I'm a boxer. I should be skipping rope and punching bags, not trying to unpick legal arguments and decipher contractual sub-clauses.

I go into this boardroom, and I sit on the same side of the table as Emanuel, and I bite my tongue. If I tell the truth about what's happening – that we never even speak, never mind see each other – that's the end of our relationship, our friendship, forever. No matter how angry and how frustrated I am, I can't bring myself to betray him like that. No matter how bad things get, the two of us should always be on the same side. So I sit there, completely hamstrung, and I say nothing. It looks like I'm coming crawling back with my tail between my legs, and I've to take my telling off like a bold child, apologise for my petulance, and move on. But Emanuel knew the truth, and I knew the truth. As soon as we step outside, I can see he's grateful that I haven't thrown him under the bus.

'Oh, those guys really went tough on you in there, Andy. Well, don't mind that.'

There's no big conversation or grand reconciliation. We both just know that I need to move back to Detroit.

'I'm going to stay here with Maud for another few days and then I'll be back next week.'

'OK, well, your room hasn't been touched. Everything's still there the way you left it.'

And that's it. By the time we return to Limerick in May 2010 to fight Mamadou Thiam, Emanuel's back in my corner. It isn't even really acknowledged that I had ever been gone. I've only been away from him for a couple of months – for one fight – but it feels like an eternity. I have to make peace with the fact that I'm never going to get all the time that I want working with Emanuel, and that some time is far better than none. Our time apart opens my eyes. New York isn't the place for me – commercialised gyms with no hunger, no edge. The Kronk is a jungle, kill or be killed. If I'm to have any chance of saving my career, that's where I need to be.

◆ ❭

I

t's good to get out of the city sometimes. We load up the car with supplies and hit the road for Chicago: me, Roger, and Daniel. It doesn't take long for the slagging and messing to start. It never does when the three of us are together.

We've been friends with Daniel since we were kids. The Fitzgeralds moved back to Limerick about a year or two after we did, and we were introduced to Daniel and his two brothers, William and Ned. We got on immediately. They liked all of the same things that we did, the Asian action films, the computer games. Daniel was the youngest of the three, a little bit younger than me and a little bit older than Roger, and he was the one that we got to know best.

It seems like he's always out visiting us in Detroit, even though that couldn't be true. When I left to come out here, Roger was at home in Limerick by himself a lot of the time, and he and Daniel became best friends, really tight. Part of the family, really. It got to a point where it wouldn't be unusual for myself and Roger to come back to the house, and Daniel would be sitting there in the kitchen, chatting away to my mam. He'd be there for hours and nobody would bat an eyelid. He'd let on that he was waiting for us to come home, but he was just as interested in using our WiFi because he didn't have any in his own place.

We wind him up a lot, but he was always the intelligent one. A real astute guy. Completely self-taught in two trades, in paving and in steelwork. When I was up in Dublin training with the amateur squad, we'd meet up a bit. Daniel was working in the city at the time, installing pipes and other equipment for Guinness.

He travels over to see me fight in America, hangs out around the gym and the house, gets to know Emanuel. Himself and Roger head off on trips around the country, and if I'm not training, I'll go with them. He's there the night I beat Belghecham in UL in November 2009, delighted that we came to him for a change rather than him coming to us.

I stick around at home for a few weeks after that fight. I go to see Matthew Macklin's fight against Rafa Sosa Pintos in the Stadium. I know a couple of the fighters on the under-card from the amateurs – Paul Hyland, Andy Murray – and RTÉ ask me to do punditry and analysis for their live TV broadcast. I make sure to get myself a good suit to wear on the night.

Roger picks me up from the train station the next day, and the three of us go out for dinner, me, him, and Daniel. Daniel's in great form, asking all about the fight and how I got on with the TV work.

'Here, that was a lovely suit you were wearing. Where did you get that from?'

A couple of days later, the Tuesday, Brian Peters asks me to go down to Cork for the day to meet some people. I get the train down from Limerick and the two of us go to pick up a sponsored car. I spend the day down there with Brian and then drive the car back up to Limerick later that evening.

I think about ringing Daniel on the way home. He loves cars, loves messing around with them, tinkering, looking at the different features of different models and thinking of ways to change them. He bought a little motorised go-kart one time and we brought it up into the mountains for a spin.

I'll give him a call and tell him that I've this new car to take a look at, I think to myself, but then I change my mind. I'm running out of credit on my phone, and I'm sure I'll see him up at the house over the next day or two anyway.

The lights are still on when I get home around eleven o'clock, which is a bit weird. Everyone would normally be in bed by now. My mam's sitting up waiting for me and she comes to open the door.

'Andy, something bad has happened. Daniel's been shot outside his uncle's place.'

Daniel was with his uncle that night when a car pulled up outside the house. He went outside to see who it was and they shot him. Daniel was never involved in any gangs or criminality. He was an innocent man shot in a case of mistaken identity. He was rushed to hospital but he died from his injuries. He was twenty-five years old.

'How's Roger?'

'He's upstairs.'

I find him in his room, lying face down on the bed, crying his eyes out. I try to console him but there's nothing to say. The words don't come any easier when I meet Noel and Teresa, Daniel's parents. They've travelled down from Belfast, where they live now, and I try to help them in whatever small way I can, offering lifts, making sure they have everything they need.

'We'll have to go and get something for him to wear. What are we going to do?'

I offer them my suit so that Daniel can be buried in it.

'He was only telling me the other day how much he liked it. I'd be honoured if you wanted to have it.'

It's only a little thing, but at least it's something I can do to help.

A few journalists ring me in the days after Daniel's death. They hear that I knew him, and ask me about my memories of him for their articles. I tell them about the bright, funny messer who became like another brother to me and Roger. A gentleman and a loyal friend. A good, innocent man who had been killed for no reason.

〈 〉

When you hurt someone, when you land the type of punch from which there's no getting up, no matter how big and brave their heart, no matter how strong their stomach for the fight, when you hit someone like that, you know it instantly. The connection is so pure, the transfer of energy from fist to foe so instantaneous, that you know they're gone before they even realise that they've been hit. Their legs wobble and then go limp, a Jenga tower in slow-motion once that final, fatal, brick has been removed. Crashing.

Freeman. Daniels. Jackson. Watch those tapes. Before they even hit the floor, I've turned away to celebrate. A sixth sense that they're gone. I don't need to stay to watch the inevitable unfold. I've written it.

When your good body shot lands, you can hear it too. The dull thud as the punch connects, and then that desperate, futile reach for breath as the muscles go into shock. You hear the air go out of them, not in the slow hiss of a burst ball, but in panicked gasps.

Then you have to press them, to take full advantage of their moment of weakness, your moment of strength, and make sure that the balance of power never finds equilibrium again. Because if you allow it, if you hesitate for just one moment, it will. In these moments, the best boxer has the instincts of a cold-blooded killer. Precise. Methodical. Completely devoid of all emotion. Utterly, utterly ruthless.

When you are strangling somebody, you have to completely overpower them. You can't let them breathe. If you apply that pressure for thirty seconds, squeeze as hard as you can, and then step back and let them catch their breath, you have to go back and do it again. And the next time, the thirty seconds will become forty seconds or fifty seconds.

When you find that punch that puts them teetering on the edge, the onus is on you then to find another one. You have to press and press and press and find a way because if you only chop one of a Hydra's heads off, two grow back. They're fighting on instinct, so you need to think about what they've seen, about what you've shown them to this point, and mix it up. Throw punches that you haven't thrown before. If you hurt them with a left hand to the body, don't go looking for that same shot again straight away like the kid who finds the biscuits in the top press. Mix it up. Headshots, headshots, headshots. Unrelenting pressure. And when the time is right, then go back to the one to finish them.

A bad fighter won't even notice his window of opportunity. He'll hurt his opponent without even knowing it. He'll step off, keep fighting the same fight on the historic terms that bound them both a few seconds ago instead of enforcing the new law that exists now. By the time he realises, typically, it's too late.

That's where a good corner man can be at his most effective. Emanuel is a great person, a great trainer, a great manager, but as a corner man, he is second to none. He understands people, so he understands fighters, and he reads me every bit as well as he reads my opponents.

When I come back to the corner, he only has a moment. I can't take in a dozen new instructions so he has to be succinct. Direct. There's time for two or three key messages, at most. One would be ideal. Every word takes energy to parse and understand so he needs to use as few as possible to leave me in no doubt as to what is important, and then let me have my rest. Communication and calmness. Emanuel knows exactly what I'm feeling, or what I'm thinking internally, and that's the message he focuses on. He articulates exactly what's going through my mind, and puts his solution forward.

I always know when my opponents are hurt because Emanuel lets me know. That's when he's at his most vocal and animated in the corner. He's switched on, watching every punch through a fighter's eyes, and when that key punch lands, he goes in for the kill as well.

'Right back, right back, right back. Go get him. Go get him. Dress him up,' he loves telling me. When you have somebody in that position where you know that you've taken their heart, it's just a matter of showing him something, a little jab to the body or a slow feint, before you go in for the finish. You've got him hurt, you've got him rocking, he's ready to go, but you have to dress him up first.

That's what makes Emanuel great. In horse racing, a good trainer will lay all the groundwork, leave no stone unturned in preparation, find the right race and plot the tactics, but when the day itself comes, you still need a good jockey to ride the horse, to take those big-picture instructions and use them as a compass as the rhythm of the race unfolds around him, to be so in tune with the horse under him and the horses around him that when the time comes to squeeze for home, he's given himself the best possible chance of getting to the line first.

A good boxing coach is the trainer and the jockey; he does both jobs.

‹ ›

Sugar Hill is in my corner the night against Craig McEwan. In my face. Very animated.

'You're losing this fight, man. You hear me? You're losing. You've got to win this fight.'

I know all this. I'm the one in there being bossed around the ring from bell to bell. I know I'm not performing. I know I'm losing. Above all else, I know what's at stake.

'Let your hands go. You're not letting your hands go.'

I've seen Emanuel go off in the corner before. I've seen him tear into the most famous fighters in the world. Jermain Taylor. Wladimir Klitschko. I've heard stories of the night Lennox Lewis left Mike Tyson in a bloody mess, and Emanuel spent the night roaring at Lewis to get him out of there, get the job done. It's not the way he likes to do things, but if he has a fighter that isn't fighting to his potential, or that isn't turning the screw when he should, he'll do what he has to do to get a reaction.

'Why are you letting him box you? You've got to start moving.'

It's all negative. It's stressing me out. Reinforcing the doubts that are in my head, rattling around with my brain every time McEwan catches me. Which is happening a lot.

If Emanuel was here, it would be praise, positivity, calmness. Start with something that I'm doing well: your jab is good, keep working that. Leave me with one message, whatever's most important: try him to the body a bit more, he doesn't like that. That's what I need now from Sugar Hill. Give me a clear instruction. Give me one word that I can focus on for the next three minutes. Give me one punch to throw. Give me something.

'Come on, man. Start throwing your punches, man. What are you doing?'

Sugar Hill is looking at me, my eyes glazed over, sitting on my stool. I've tuned out. Lost in worry. He can't get any response.

———

Later that night, I'm in the dressing room, decompressing. Jim Strickland comes and sits down beside me. He's a legend of the sport. Trainer, manager, cutman. When Emanuel realised he couldn't be here, he asked Jim to come in his place. Sugar Hill is the number one on the night. He's the man who is with me day in, day out in the gym, the man who knows me best, with the exception of Emanuel. But when Jim stands in your corner, he brings years of experience with him. A softly spoken man, which at first seems a bit unusual for someone involved in boxing, until you get to know him and understand that he doesn't often need to raise his voice because when he speaks, you listen.

I'm shattered and sore and I just want a few minutes by myself to unwind. Jim saw what we all saw out there. He knows it's not the time for a lecture, but he also knows that this needs to be addressed, so he does it quickly.

'All that stuff in the corner, the shouting and the hollering, that does you no good.'

He tells Sugar Hill the same thing. What you're going through in the ring is a battle. When you come back to your corner, it shouldn't be a battle as well. That's your rest, your reprieve, your sanctuary. A place where you can recuperate.

A place of peace.

———

The road to a world title shot was supposed to go through John Duddy, not Craig McEwan. So be it.

People have been putting my name and Duddy's together since I turned pro. Barstool matchmaking. It doesn't take much imagination or ingenuity to pair off the two Irish middleweights in America and see which one is left standing. Duddy with a few years more experience, me as the new kid on the block, and there's only room for one of us to reach the top.

It's not that we've been avoiding each other. Far from it. It's just that whenever this fight happens, we'll both be putting it all on the line, so the risk has to match that reward, and it never has. Until now.

There's always been too much to lose. Now I've nothing to lose. Neither does he. He had his chance against Julio César Chávez Jr and couldn't take it. He needs a front-page win to put himself back in the picture. I'm the one standing in his way if he wants to get back for a second shot.

I'll take my chances wherever they come at the moment. Two-bit fights against journeymen with no profile aren't going to pay any bills, and they're definitely not going to turn any heads or move me up in the rankings. At my most optimistic, I tell myself to be patient, that there's more to it than meaningless fight after meaningless fight, that I'm staying busy while keeping free. But there's only a whim of the current between floating and floundering.

HBO make the fight. March 12th 2011 in the MGM Grand at Foxwoods Resort, a casino on a Native American reservation in a place called Mashantucket, Connecticut. The chief support bout on the undercard when Sergio Martínez – the man we all have to beat and quite possibly the best pound-for-pound boxer in the world right now – fights Sergiy Dzinziruk.

Now that we both want it, it's an easy fight to sell. We both have our fans, and we both have the styles to put on a show. Duddy with his reputation as a walk-forward warrior; me, the considered counterpuncher. They're calling it Irish War, a derby fight on the weekend before St Patrick's Day. Emanuel is happy to play up the hype. He's talking about it as the biggest all-Irish fight in decades.

But the fight never happens. Our camp has already started when we hear the news. Duddy has retired. Left his $100,000 purse on the table and walked away for good. He's open and honest about his reasons. He doesn't have the hunger. The fire has burned out. I totally understand. Everyone's day comes; someday mine will too. But where does it leave me now?

HBO start their search for Duddy's replacement, and Craig McEwan is the name they arrive at: an unbeaten Scottish fighter, 19–0, trained by Freddie Roach. A southpaw too. I know him. I've beaten him. It was back in 2005, when I thought I was staying amateur. I fought him in the Four Nations final and I was comfortably better than him. It's not 2005 any more though, and I have to remember that.

We fly to Florida for the final weeks of the training camp. It's Miguel Cotto's camp, really. He's fighting in Las Vegas on the same night as me, defending his belt against Ricardo Mayorga. Emanuel brings a lot of his best fighters down. He wants the standard set at the highest possible level, everybody trying to impress, pushing each other in the gym and sparring.

I've waited five years to make my debut on HBO. I'm under no illusions what this means and in no way complacent about the threat McEwan will bring. He'll try to box me at my own game, to move and to counter, and hope that I run out of patience before he runs out of legs. I know I need to be fully focused, but it's next to impossible when the phone keeps ringing.

It's Damian. Or it's Perry. Or somebody else. I'm not the only one who has been getting frustrated over the last two years as we meandered along the road to nowhere. Perry and the investment group have been pumping in cash to keep the show on the road. For a lot of these fights, they're not only paying me my monthly stipend, funding my training camp, all of my expenses, and paying my sparring partners; they're also putting up the purse for an opponent to come and fight me. They're not running out of cash, but they are running out of patience, and unless there's a big fight in my future – even a roadmap to a big fight – they're wasting their time.

They've been holding talks and taking meetings in the background, and they come to us with a plan. They've negotiated a deal with Lou DiBella, and it's in everyone's best interests that I sign it and officially join up with DiBella Entertainment as my promoter. I'm hesitant. I know Emanuel doesn't like these kinds of deals. He thinks they're too restrictive, they tie your hands. He is adamant that it's much better to be a free agent, to let your fighting do the talking, and be so in demand that promoters are coming to you. You don't have to take fights that you don't want, and if you do want the fight, you're immediately starting with a much stronger hand when it comes to negotiating.

When he hears that the investors have been holding talks without him, he flips.

'Ignore them, you don't need a deal with DiBella. We'll get you the big fights, trust me. Whatever you do, do not sign that contract.'

It's like a cross-continental phone relay. Perry in Chicago rings Damian in Belfast. Lou DiBella is going to pull Andy from the HBO fight unless the contract is signed before then. He needs to stop dragging his feet and just do it. It's all or nothing now. They want to bind themselves to DiBella Entertainment, so either take the deal, or they're voiding their management contract with me and pulling the funding.

Damian in Belfast rings me in Florida, and all I want is for a few uninterrupted hours where I can focus on my training. But if this doesn't get sorted and the fight gets pulled, I'm training for nothing anyway. So I take the call, and Damian passes on the message.

When I go home that evening, I have to talk to Emanuel about it because he's staying next door to me in the same apartment complex. But he's not for turning.

'DiBella can't take you off that card, Andy. It's a HBO card, HBO are the ones paying the purse, so if they want you to fight, you'll be fighting. They're just trying to scare you. This fight's happening, don't worry.'

Once upon a time, I would have taken Emanuel's word as gospel, but I know him now, and I know that's he more than capable of a few sleights of hand, a white lie or two, if it's in his interest or if he thinks it serves the greater good. Every time I ring Maud and try to make sense of the latest dribble of information, I can hear her getting more and more frustrated. Somebody is trying to play me here, she's sure of it. She's just not sure who it is.

I trust Damian to give it to me straight, the way he always has since day one. We talk it through. Maybe we've been standing at a crossroads all this time without fully appreciating it. I don't have to sign the deal, but if that's the path I choose, I have to be comfortable with the possibility that in two years' time I'll still be on a road trip through middle America fighting faceless journeymen. If I sign it, I'll get the fight against McEwan, make my HBO debut, and if I win, it will be the springboard that I need to finally move into title conversation, to a shot at Martínez. If I lose, I'm screwed. I'm tied into Lou DiBella for the foreseeable future and there's no chance that he'll keep pushing me as a legitimate challenger with two defeats on my record. I'll be back to small halls and midweek nights for the rest of my career. I might as well be finished. But then again, if I don't sign it and lose, I'm screwed anyway.

I finally make my mind up, a week before the fight. For all of the talk and the threats, nobody has pulled the plug. But I have to put my faith in myself, in my own two gloves, and take my chances. I have to sign it.

Emanuel calls me that morning while I'm on my way out to the gym for my final session of the camp. He's already gone to Vegas with Cotto, but he just wants to let me know where he stands one last time. Unequivocally.

'If you sign that contract, it is the worst decision you will ever make.'

I say nothing. I've already made my mind up. I'm not re-considering. Until something happens to make me do just that.

I get in for my final sparring session. I'm paired up with Demetrius Andrade, a young unbeaten light-middleweight scrambling up a ladder to the stars two rungs at a time. He clips me just above the eye and, a few moments later, backs off me and slows down. Shit, man, you're bleeding. I let Sugar Hill take a look, and then I go to check it out in the mirror for myself. The skin is broken, but it's hard to tell how deep the cut is. Bad enough that if I showed up to the weigh-in or on fight night with it looking as fresh as it is now, there's no way a doctor would clear me to fight. Maybe not so bad that it won't have healed in a week. It's hard to tell. I'm worried though. If I sign this contract, and the fight is called off because of the cut, I've tied myself to DiBella Entertainment for nothing. Maybe it's a sign. Maybe I should let it go.

I call Damian again.

'I've been cut in sparring this morning but it doesn't look that bad. It looks like I'll probably be OK to fight. What do you think I should do about the contract?'

'If you think you'll be OK, I'd go ahead and sign it.'

I'm restless for the entire journey as Sugar Hill drives me over to the office of Leon Margules, the famous boxing lawyer, in Fort Lauderdale. Even after I've signed it and there's no going back, I'm still uneasy until I call Emanuel to tell him. He takes a deep breath.

'You've made a bad mistake.'

It's no different from what he's been saying to me this entire time but now his words land like lead in the pit of my stomach. Maybe I should have trusted him this whole time.

'Well, OK, fuck it. Let's just get on with it, Andy. You've signed the contract now. There's nothing we can do about that. We'll just make it work.'

That's what you're going to tell me now, after weeks of torture, after sitting there and happily letting me believe that this was life or death, that everything was on the line, that my career and everything that we've been working towards for the last five years would be undone if we made the wrong decision here. I'm making my HBO debut in a few days, the biggest fight of my career, and I haven't been able to focus on my training in weeks because every moment of concentration has been interrupted with the *ping-ping-ping* of my phone.

At least it's over now. Fuck it. Let's just get on with it.

——

I throw a left to the body but McEwan is wise to it and gets low to cover up well. But in the blink that it takes him to come out of his crouch and bounce back into an upright position, I catch him flush with a right full of power. He staggers. I've tested him early and he's passed, but I've laid down my marker now. The fight is less than a minute old.

I win that first round convincingly, and I think I have this guy's number. I controlled him as an amateur, and now I'm drunk on the success of my first good punch in the fight. I go out in the second to do it again, to find the big shot that will finish him, but in my haste, I forget the basics and I leave the door open; McEwan steps right through. He changes his tactics, works behind his jab a bit more. Starts to box.

He wins the second round.

The third.

The fourth.

Now I'm starting to panic.

When you step into the ring, your preparation always plays out in the fight. If you've ticked all the boxes in your physical training, been meticulous with your diet, and thought through every scenario from a tactical point of view, it will all be reflected in your performance as you hoped it would. But if you cut corners or let your standards drop, you won't be able to hide that either.

We leave Florida and fly to Connecticut a few days before the fight: me, Sugar Hill, Joey, and Roger. Every team needs a leader, and because Emanuel is not there, I have to step up and take on that responsibility. I'm comfortable being in control but when you're the designated point man, the go-to guy, you've got to deal with everything. All of the decisions are passed along the line. Ask Andy what time we're training at. Ask Andy where we're going to eat tonight. And then I'm the one who has to tell everybody where they need to go and when we have to be there. Half-past seven in the morning for breakfast. This room at this time for the fighters' meeting. Then we've to meet the doctor. And don't forget the publicity meeting. On top of that, the tax people contact me and politely inform me that I'm not a resident according to their records, so they'll be withholding a huge chunk of the money from my purse on the night. I get that sorted, but it's the ordeal you'd expect.

There's always something: 'Andy, front desk rang there. They need a credit card. Will you go down and give them yours'?

Sergio Martínez is not doing all of these things during fight week. I doubt Craig McEwan is either. They have people to do it for them. I do it because someone has to, but then I get snappy when things to don't run to plan. I have a row with Sugar Hill, frustrated because he has us hanging around waiting, and then I have to apologise when I realise that it has just been a miscommunication. I'm on edge. They're all minor inconveniences when you take them in isolation, things that most people routinely have to deal with on a daily basis while going about their normal, functioning lives. But it all accumulates, and when you're days out from a fight, you need to conserve all of the energy that it's slowly leaching away.

It all comes out in your performance. The stress with the contract, the disorganisation of the camp, it's all magnified tenfold. Every fighter has to endure pain. Some have to endure more than others. The best fighters are the ones who are able to push their threshold to the limit and withstand the pain, to think logically and clearly in spite of it.

I can't get my thoughts together, compose myself, think freely, box freely. Sugar Hill is aggressive, doing everything he can to get through to me. All I can think is that this fight is slipping away from me, round by round, a car crash in slow motion that I'm powerless to stop. It has taken me years to get here, but if I lose, it's all over. The contract with DiBella will mean nothing. I'll never get back to this level again, never get a shot at a world title. I might as well retire. It's over. My career is over.

McEwan doesn't need to be inside my head in order to take advantage. I'm barely boxing. It's all one-way traffic and all I can I do is survive. Apart from the first, I haven't won another round clearly. Maybe I did just enough to sneak one or two others, but if this goes the distance, I haven't a prayer. He's already won.

———

Maud sits on the edge of the bed and turns the volume up again. Every few seconds, a figure passes by the open door of the hotel room, pacing the corridor. Zoe, her sister. Zoe had been in the arena, watched the first few rounds, and left. It was too much. Maud didn't even make it that far. Her ticket sits in her handbag, the stub untorn.

She turns it up and Jim Lampley, the HBO commentator, narrates her worst nightmare, puts life and death in black and white.

If Andy Lee loses this fight, he'll have nothing.

Nothing. So extreme, so dramatic, so brutally plausible. She screams at the TV, the first banalities that come into her head, willing me, imploring me. Jab. Move. Hit him. Do something.

She reaches her hand out to touch the screen. Zoe walks by again.

———

I've nothing left to lose. In another nine minutes, I'll have lost it all anyway. That thought crystallises in a moment of pure clarity. An epiphany. No, I think to myself. If he wants to beat me, if he wants to take it all away from me, let him kill me.

With my hands tight to my head, I start to walk forward. He's still unloading at will but there's a shift in the dynamic. I'm taking his punches, on my arms and on my gloves, but physically I'm closing down that space between us, forcing him backwards with my presence, making him adjust his feet if he wants to keep creating angles, finding shots.

For the first time since the opening round, I'm asserting myself, even if I'm not throwing any punches of my own.

That's the next step. I start to jab, and then to throw in pairs. One-two. One-two. One-two. They don't all land cleanly, but some of them do, enough to introduce a little bit of doubt in his mind, to make him feel like his grasp on the fight is slowly being pried loose, and that's enough for now. Maybe I've done enough to nick that round, maybe not, but what matters is the perception. In the championship rounds, when a fight's on the line, even the smallest shift in momentum can seem like an avalanche.

I stick to the same plan in the ninth, chip away at his control. Both of us are tiring. Even the clean punches don't have the same power anymore. I make a few count, but when he loads up in return, he's hitting fresh air. A big left hand whistles past as I spin onto the ropes. Millimetres. He holds me, letting the last minute of this round tick away for as long as possible. It's smart, but it lets me dictate the next exchange. When we break, he's slightly off balance and I catch him on the back foot. The jab sets it up, and I slam him straight down the middle with my left. He staggers backwards as his legs crumple, slumped in the corner as the referee picks up the count.

I have him. I know I have him. When I go back to the corner for the final time, the atmosphere has completely changed. It's all positive reinforcement.

'That's it, that's it, you've done it now. Let your hands go.'

I keep it simple, the exact same strategy that has brought me back to life. One-two straight. One-two straight. He's living the longest three minutes of his life, starting to unravel, and it won't take much. I throw a quick jab, barely there, but it's the straight left that hits like a sledgehammer. He lashes back and leaves himself wide open for a right hook planted on his jawline. He can't hang on. He knows he can't.

One last left leaves him on his knees. The referee crouches over him, telling him it's all going to be alright.

I kneel and bless myself, and when I get back to my feet, it's pure pandemonium in the ring. I don't know what Sugar Hill is saying to me but it sure sounds good. Roger grabs me, kisses me on the side of the head. I look out into the crowd for Maud and instead I see my mam, the cameras chasing her as she runs down to ringside, the happiness, the relief as she waves her tricolour.

I see her, and I give her a little wink. Don't worry. It's all OK now.

———

He probably thinks about those last two rounds every day. If he could just have held on, if he could just have gathered his resolve, thought about it, took a breath, he would have won the fight.

I know exactly how he feels. I've felt it before.

I reach out to him when I'm in Edinburgh a few years later. He's back home living in Scotland with his family. Golden Boy put him in against Kid Chocolate, Peter Quillin, in his very next fight. On the back of losing to me, they matched him against one of the most dangerous middleweights in the world, 25–0 with nineteen knockouts. When he lost, they lost interest, and he went back to fighting in the UK.

I send him a message when I'm in town, see if he wants to catch up, but he's not available.

I think about him often.

‹ ›

Once I notice the cut above Brian Vera's eye, the first trickle of red seeping through the strands of eyebrow, it's all I can think about. Another clash of heads, the same as the first fight, except this time he's the one who comes off second best, not me. That's karma for you, although it would be nice if justice had seen fit to take its natural course a little bit more promptly; three and a half years is an awful long time to wait. Sugar Hill has taught me well, and if you're a smart fighter, you don't need to be a dirty fighter. I concentrate my jab on that one spot. Hard, solid blows. I see him wincing, and I like it. There's a sick pleasure in seeing each fresh spurt of blood.

There's nothing personal between me and Vera. This rematch, it's just something that I've got to do.

I'll always have unfinished business until I avenge that defeat. I'll never be able to truly move on until I right that wrong. I made my peace with that fact a long time ago; once I've done that, I just have to wait my turn. Emanuel puts big offers on the table to arrange a second fight, much bigger than Vera is getting elsewhere, but he's pushed back every time. Time goes by, and time heals, but it doesn't change what happened. It doesn't erase the loss from my record, doesn't cover over that blemish. Nothing can. Redemption is the best I can hope for now, and that can only come in the ring.

This time, there'll be no mistakes. Once the fight is booked, I move to Chicago with Roger for a month, and I spend all of that time working with a strength and conditioning trainer. Vera might have been the tougher, heavier man the first time we fought but I leave nothing to chance this time around. I try to understand him, this big, tough Texan brawler that doesn't seem bothered by anything. It's like the two of us are from different planets. He's a very limited fighter, but he seems almost unaware of his limitations. Oblivious. Maybe that's what you need to succeed. I dwell on every little detail, but Vera, he just turns up and fights. He doesn't let the million little doubts and thoughts undermine him.

I remember meeting up with Zaur Antia when I was back in Ireland after the first fight. We went for a walk by the sea in Bray, and all of this was clearly playing on my mind.

'Do you think it's an advantage or disadvantage being an intelligent person and a boxer? Do those two things go hand in hand, or is there a conflict there?'

Zaur didn't hesitate. 'It's not about an advantage or disadvantage. You have to be very, very intelligent to be a good boxer.'

A good boxer can think clearly and fluidly under sustained pressure, stay in control of his situation and stay in control of himself, process his environment and his opponent, and perform, all at the same time. Intelligence is a prerequisite, not an optional extra. I knew Zaur was right – I knew it without even asking the question – but I had so many doubts at that moment that I couldn't see it for myself.

This time I win by a distance, and when I meet Vera and his brother out in the stands afterwards, there's nothing but respect between us. He jokes about another rematch to complete the trilogy but I'm finished with this chapter of my life and ready for the next one. Below us in the ring, Sergio

Martínez defends his titles against Darren Barker in the main event. Now it's my turn.

I've already waited long enough. After I beat McEwan, Martínez should have been next, but instead, my performance that night put me back on ice again. For a long time, I was annoyed with myself, furious that I had let another chance slip through my fingers, not appreciating the incredible strength I'd shown that night to pull it out of the fire and save myself: the heart, the courage, the determination. It was an entertaining fight, Lou DiBella said afterwards, but it proved that I wasn't ready for a title shot yet. After my performance against Vera, he can have no more arguments.

All that's left is to set the time and the date, and then boxing teaches me another one of its many cruel lessons: the fight is never signed until it's signed, and even then, don't bank on it. Me, Emanuel, the Chicago guys – we trust that that we will be looked after, and we're all outflanked. Brian Peters outmanoeuvres us. He negotiates a deal between Matthew Macklin and DiBella Entertainment, and Macklin jumps to the top of the queue and lands the jackpot in his first fight: a world title shot against Martínez on St Patrick's Day 2012 in Madison Square Garden.

My consolation prize is a slot on the undercard. They fly me to New York and take media shots for posters, and there's still no mention of who my opponent might be. I'm by myself at that first press conference; Emanuel is unable to travel, and the Chicago guys can't make it either, so I ring Keith Sullivan, my lawyer, and ask him to come as an advisor so I'm not sitting there by myself twiddling my thumbs while Martínez and Macklin get to work selling their fight.

I'm promised the chief support slot again, but I nearly fall out of my chair when I find out who they're trying to line up as my opponent. It's HBO's card and they're insisting that I fight Peter Quillin. That's a Grade A matchup, the kind that would pack out an arena on its own. Quillin's an unbeaten fighter, a real puncher. He would arguably give Martínez a tougher test than Macklin would. It's much too big a fight to be made for an undercard. We go back to them with an alternative, propose Brian Magee to add some all-Irish flavour to the card for the weekend that's in it but HBO don't want to know. We try to negotiate, suggest Giovanni Lorenzo as another alternative, put forward a whole list of potential opponents, but they won't budge.

Part of me wants to take the fight against Quillin; I'm confident that I can beat him, and if I do, there'll be no way to deny me a title shot in my next fight. But I know what their play is here. I know that I'm being used. While Macklin's been at home in Ireland and the UK, I'm the one who has been fighting up and down along the East Coast: New York, New Jersey, Connecticut, Massachusetts. I'm the Irish fighter with the American audience. They know I'll be the draw. They'll know I'll sell tickets. But yet Macklin is the one who gets the title fight, and Martínez gets the easier defence. It's totally disrespectful.

They offer me $100,000 to take the fight, but there are bigger things in life than money. I keep seeing the opportunity in it, and I'm afraid that I might damage my relationship with HBO, but even taking all of that into account, I'm not going to sell myself to them for a pay cheque, and that's exactly what I'd be doing. I turn them down.

Instead of fighting in front of five thousand people in Madison Square Garden on St Patrick's Day, I fight a week earlier in the Suburban Collection Showplace in a little city called Novi, just outside of Detroit. Emanuel organises a card and puts on his own local show so that I can keep busy, have a fight, have a win. I stop Saul 'Baby' Duran, a veteran Mexican journeyman, early in the second round. When I collect the purse for my night's work, it comes to about $7,000.

They hung their bodies, nine of them, from a bridge over the freeway in Nuevo Laredo in Mexico. Police found fourteen severed heads in coolers outside the city hall a few hours later. Retaliation. The corpses, what was left of them, were stuffed in black plastic bags in an abandoned car near the border.

I know I'm going into the lion's den long before I look out of the window of the little propeller plane that's taking us down to the city of El Paso, tucked away right on the border between the US and Mexico. There's nothing to see, no sign of life, only desert. In the distance, I spot a little ranch lost in the wasteland; I won't see another one for fifteen minutes.

The first time that I flew down here, before these latest atrocities, they announced that the fight had to be moved for fear that the conflict could spill over into America. We stood on the 50-yard line in the Sun Bowl stadium, me and Julio César Chávez Jr, the WBC middleweight champion, holding a press conference for a fight that seemingly had no venue. A move to San Antonio, still in the heart of Chávez country but placid by comparison, was suggested. Emanuel smiled at me.

'Andy, someone always seems to be looking out for you, you know.'

A week later, the fight was back on again. The drug cartels let it be known that there was a temporary truce, that the stadium would be declared a neutral zone for the night. Their war continued elsewhere; a week after the venue was confirmed, the bodies and the heads were found.

Statistically, El Paso is the safest city in America, and all of the locals that I've met seem lovely, but I don't want to be here. The promoters are promising that there'll be thirty thousand people inside that stadium, and I know that I'll be able to count the amount of them that are there to support me on my fingers. If I'm lucky, it might stretch to a few toes too. But I've been waiting forever for my world title shot, and I've always known that when it came, it wouldn't be on my terms.

I've had twenty-nine fights as a professional and, in theory at least, every one of them has been a move to plot my way into this position. A six-year-long game of chess, even if it has felt a lot more like snakes and ladders at times. The great irony is that when the call finally comes, it's not because we've been shrewd and I've been cleverly managed into position. It's pure luck. By rights, this is Martin Murray's fight. He's the one pushed into the picture after holding Felix Sturm to a draw; he's the one that the Chávez camp agree to face. Murray signs the contract. They set a date: June 16th 2012. But there's a delay with Murray's visa, an issue because he spent time in prison when he was younger, and he has to pull out.

And when they run through the list of contenders in the middleweight division in search of a replacement, they land on me. Chávez has already beaten Zbik, Manfredo, and Rubio. Barker and Macklin have both lost to Martínez within the last year. They don't even want to consider a unification bout between the two champions right now. I'm ranked, and I'm unbeaten in my last thirteen fights. I'm in.

For the first time in my life, I'm the challenger. The B side. And that means I have to put up with B side treatment. I know that's the deal; it doesn't make it any less disgusting. They do everything they can to undermine you, and there's no shame or pretence. They want to leave you under no illusion that everything is stacked against you. They want you to feel like there's no way you can win a fair fight. Fairness left town a long time ago. Fight week is a long week, and when you're sitting in your hotel room, relaxing, recovering, preparing, they want all of these little moves to be gnawing away at your confidence until you're completely demoralised.

We're under no illusions from the moment the contract is signed. I'm not going to walk into Chávez's back yard, scrape a narrow points decision, and leave, blowing kisses, with his belt slung over my shoulder. Nobody's naive enough to think that will happen. I need to knock him out. At the very least, I need to be decisive.

We're anticipating every trick in the book that Chávez's camp might try to throw at us, but that doesn't necessarily mean we can avoid them. We control what we can. Top Rank offer to book our hotel for us. We swerve that. We can look after ourselves. We find a nice place outside the city, a good bit away, where we can be relatively anonymous. I book all of my friends and family into the same hotel. When you're up against it, you keep your allies as close as possible.

But from the start of the week, we're already on the back foot. Emanuel's not there. He's in Austria, in camp with Wladimir to help him get ready for his rematch with Tony Thompson. He assures me that he will be there, that he's on the end of the phone whenever we need him, and that Sugar Hill knows exactly what to do until he arrives. We won't even miss him. I remember those first conversations we had, how Emanuel promised me that I would be his world champion.

Now we're a few days away from that moment and he's on the other side of the world. This wasn't what we agreed. This wasn't the plan. If he truly believed in those words, that prophecy, he'd be here. It knocks my confidence a little.

I'm determined that whatever strokes they pull, nothing will knock me out of my stride, and just as importantly, that they see that their games aren't working. They arrange a public workout for me early in the week but pick a place way out on the outskirts. We're in the car for over an hour, the Texas sun doing its level best to melt us. When we get there, there's a few media people waiting, some local kids running around, and that's it.

I fulfil every obligation that's asked of me; I barely see Chávez all week. But in the back of my mind, I know that if Emanuel was here with us, he wouldn't let them get away with any of this. They wouldn't even try in the first place.

On the morning of the weigh-in, I'm six pounds over. Emanuel always likes us to maintain as much of our weight as possible right up until the last minute but that's too much. I need to get to work. I get dressed in the heaviest clothes I can find and go down to the car park to start running. The sun has only just come up and it's still hotter than the hottest summer's day in Ireland, 30°C at least. I do laps, shuttles, sprints, anything that will help me to work up a sweat, to get these last six pounds to evaporate right off my skin. I go back to my room and check the scales again. Nowhere near enough. They would disappear off me in a sauna – they always do – but that's about the only thing missing from this hotel. I go into the bathroom, turn the shower and the taps on as hot as they will go, and let them run. I lock the door, and as the room around me fills with steam, I start shadow boxing. I up the tempo, quicker and quicker, until my heart is pumping and I'm drenched. When I step up onto the scales a few hours later, and stare out blankly into a sea of Chávez fans, I'm three-quarters of a pound under the limit. Chávez comes in at 159lbs. The fight is on.

I'm tired, I'm cranky, I'm massively dehydrated, and on top of all of that, I haven't eaten a proper meal in days. I start slowly sipping on the drinks that I brought with me to get some fluids back on board. Chávez already has a plate of food in his hand. We didn't bring any with us, and now all I want is to get back to the hotel so that I can have something to eat.

There's an argument, and Perry's right there in the middle of it. He hasn't been here all week either. He only flew in this morning with a big crew on his private jet and immediately started telling me how he was here to set things straight.

'We're here for you, Andy. We won't let nothing go on. We won't let no dirty tricks go on.'

He's not happy with the gloves. He produces this weighing scales from I don't know where and starts weighing my gloves there in full view of everyone. Ten ounces, as you'd expect. Then he looks to Top Rank to do the same for Chávez's. I don't know if there's anything going on with the gloves, if they've any reason to be suspicious, but this is the fight they've chosen to pick on my behalf and they're not backing down. Top Rank laugh in their faces. The Texas state athletic commission want nothing to do with it. Perry goes directly to Freddie Roach, Chávez's trainer, but he's not interested in the slightest. The gloves never get weighed.

We leave the circus and get out of there, but we've barely arrived back in the hotel when there's another issue.

'We need to go back into the city.'

'Why?'

'They need us to come back. They said you need to see the doctor.'

'Tell them I saw the doctor.'

'I did. They said you didn't get a full check-up so they need you to come back.'

Whatever patience I had left is long gone by now. The last thing I need is to spend another half-hour sitting in traffic in this sweltering heat. We go under duress – we've no other option – and when we get there, they seem quite happy to tell us that it's all been cleared up and the doctor's gone home now but thanks for coming all the way back in anyway.

Emanuel arrives on the morning of the fight. I'm delighted to see him, and still not quite over the fact that he has been on the other side of the world all week while I've been getting messed around. He's had a marathon journey to get here: a two-hour drive from the camp in Austria to Munich airport, and then two or three flights to get from Munich to El Paso in time. He could have made an excuse and not come at all but he wanted to be here. At the time I didn't know how sick he was; maybe he didn't either.

That evening, we arrive early. I can imagine what this place is like when it's full with fifty thousand fans packed in for a college football game. There won't be anything like that number tonight. Ticket sales have been slow. Maybe it will work to my advantage. They show us to our dressing room. I'm expecting one of the big football locker rooms that can comfortably hold seventy or eighty people. Wishful thinking. They must have moved the brooms to make space for us in the cupboard that they give us instead. It's barely big enough to stand in, never mind get changed. We measure it out. Six foot by twelve.

We can't stay there, so I grab Roger and the two of us go to check out the arena, our usual routine. Halfway down the walkway, he turns and looks at me. 'Small ring.'

Yeah. It's tiny, sixteen foot, when a championship ring should be at least twenty-one foot, twenty-three foot. There's nothing in the rules to stop them, and this is perfect for Chávez. He wants to draw me into a firefight. He wants me to stand there and trade with him. That's his style. The bigger the ring, the more space I'll have to box and move. They cut that advantage off at the source.

We go back to our broom cupboard to get ready. Emanuel wraps my hands, I put my gloves on, and we start warming up. Half an hour before ring walk, there's a knock on the door. The drug testers. They had the whole night to do this – they could even wait and do it afterwards. I'm sure it's no coincidence that they've waited until I'm fully in the zone, ready to go.

I'm not going to roll over here, not when I'm about to step into the ring with a man who has already failed a drug test and served a seven-month suspension for using a banned diuretic. Chávez fails another test in September 2012, a few months after we fight – he gets a nine-month ban and a $900,000 fine, though that's later reduced to $100,000.

'Is he being made do this? Are you going to ask him to take a piss?'

'Yeah, he's doing it now.'

'I want one of my guys to see it to make sure he does it.'

Sugar Hill goes to observe, and when he comes back, he has a quiet look about him. He says nothing and I don't press him on it. It's not the time. This man is an ex-Detroit police officer. He knows how to read a room, read a situation, so when he eventually explains to me, I know he's sceptical about what he saw.

'I went into the room and there was a guy coming out with the piss bottle in his hands. Chávez was standing over the other side of the room, and they were all laughing.'

The next time there's a knock on the door, it's showtime. I don't hear the boos, the whistles, but I know they're there. I can feel the canvas, soft beneath my feet, as soon as I step up into the ring. Like a mattress. Another play in Chávez's favour. The more I move, the quicker my legs are going to burn out on a canvas with this much give.

I box him in that first round, just the way we planned. Light on my feet. Working my jab. There's no doubt that I'm the better, more skilled fighter here. I win the round. Back in the corner, it's all positive from Emanuel. It's beautiful, he tells me. Keep it going, keep controlling him. If he tries to force it, stay relaxed. Sooner or later, you'll catch him with something.

Emanuel tells me that Chávez won the second round, but the third was definitely mine. By the end of the fourth, I feel like I've done enough to win all four. He catches me a few times in that fourth. I'm wide open for one of his right hands. He gets in on top of me and I don't even see the left uppercut that follows. Emanuel reminds me what's at stake.

'Get yourself together, man. Talk to yourself. This is it. There ain't no second chance.'

He sees the exact same dangers that I can see. Box him. Box him. You're ahead when you box him. But I can't keep the distance between us. Chávez is starting to lean on me, using his size to put me under pressure. We feared this might happen. In his last few fights, he's somehow managed to put 20lbs back on overnight between the weigh-in and fight. All through this camp, I've been going out to an ice rink in the suburbs of Detroit to train with Britta Ottoboni, a brilliant figure-skating strength and conditioning coach. We brought in the biggest middleweights we could find for sparring, and a few fighters that were even bigger again, more natural super-middleweights – Edwin Rodriguez, Donovan George. We bring in Vera too. I feel like I'm in there against a 185-pounder; I was only back up at 170lbs when we checked in the dressing room, so if that's right, he's a full stone heavier than me, and he's making it work for him. It's a huge factor. I could be the best middleweight in the world but a half-decent heavyweight would push me around the ring like a plaything, like an adult putting his hand on a little kid's head while the kid swings away wildly and misses every time.

I can't hold him off, and that's why I start to panic. I'm a Kronk fighter. Long-range. Hard-hitting. Explosive. Looking for a knockout. All of those things. Fighting up close, on the inside, has never really been something that we prioritised in training. We work on tying people up and moving them to the centre of the ring instead. Any time someone gets close to me, there's an internal panic. All thought and strategy go out the window. Hit him, hit him, or hold him until the referee calls break, just to get him off me.

It has worked for me in my fights up until now, but Chávez is better than anyone I've ever faced, and I can feel that it's not working. It might only be a foot or two in size but that space between us, that's what will decide this fight. That's what Emanuel means when he says box: stay off the ropes, draw him back into the centre of the ring, preserve that distance at all costs. But right now Chávez is able to cross that line at will, dictate how close he gets, and hurt me when he gets there. He's cutting me off at every turn, lording the advantages of the heavy man in the small ring. That internal panic, that stress, eats into your energy stores. And now I'm taking his shots. They're not hurting me but he's landing a lot and I'm struggling to find some sort of meaningful reply.

I knew it all coming in. I knew he weighed heavy. I knew that they were going to pull every dirty trick to give him the advantage. I knew that was the deal I had signed up for but I wasn't good enough to handle it, to win despite them. I let it affect my confidence. I let it demoralise me.

He seems impervious to my punches, like they're being glanced away by a forcefield. He backs me up against the ropes in the seventh and unloads, and for less than a moment, I realise that I don't want to win this fight. This isn't sport. There's nothing honourable or decent about this. This is not what I've been dreaming of. They can keep their tainted belt. Fucking keep it. I've given everything to get this shot – I've earned it – and now that I'm here, I've been cheated. Nothing about this fight has been fair. It has never been fought on an even keel. Money means everything to them. I should want it more, to give these people the ultimate two fingers, but I don't. Fucking keep the lot of it.

The referee steps between us and waves his arms.

LONDON

‹ ›

When I wake up, it's just like any other morning except this is not any other day. Today, tonight, I will be world champion. It's the first thing that pops into my head, before I'm even conscious of being fully awake. The thought of it, that's what wakes me.

But apart from that, it's like any other morning. There's a current of excitement that's not there when you're pulling on the gym gear and runners at 7am and heading out on the road, but that's the only outlier of emotion. No nerves. Maud is beside me, still fast asleep. When she wakes, we'll have breakfast. She already has it prepared, the hotel room fridge stocked, the portion sizes measured out. Nothing left up to chance, especially not today.

I wait for her to wake, so I close my eyes again and I hear Adam's voice. When the gap closes, don't wait. Get low. Get in close. Do the work, shut him down, tie him up. Wait for the referee to break you, then get away from him and get back to where you want to be. It's not about winning those moments. It's about making sure he doesn't get control.

A day like this will never come again but I'm ready for it. I'm sure of it. I know what it means to be an Adam Booth fighter. I've fully embraced everything that he is teaching me. Bought in 100 per cent. It couldn't have worked any other way. My body feels different. The training has transformed it. I sit lower in my legs now. My punches are more explosive, more powerful. The changes didn't click immediately but now this new way of fighting comes as naturally to me as

anything I learned in Detroit. It's a part of who I am. Built in
the Kronk, finessed in London.

Vegas feels right. The place where Emanuel slowly,
subconsciously, introduced me to being a champion. I look
out the window, go out onto the balcony, and see Caesar's
Palace across the road, where he was king on so many
historic nights. I think about what he'd say to me now if he
was standing here beside me on the morning of the fight. I
miss him deeply, think about him every day. I'll do it tonight.
I'll do it for him.

———

After the Chávez fight, I take a break, fly to London to do
some TV work at the Olympics and to spend time with
Maud. Scrolling through my phone absent-mindedly, I see
the news for the very first time. An announcement from
HBO on Twitter. Our regular analyst Emanuel Steward won't
be with us this week as he is unwell, but he will be back in
the booth for our next broadcast.

That doesn't sound like Emanuel at all. He would never
miss a fight on HBO unless it was completely unavoidable.
This is a man who lives by the red-eye timetable, flying across
the country at crazy hours to call fights and still make sure
that he's back in the gym the next morning before anyone
can miss him. He loves that job, and he doesn't allow himself
to get sick; he just puts the head down and carries on until
whatever ache or pain or illness gets bored and gives up.

It's no secret that he's sixty-eight, but when he's in public,
he acts like the thirty-something he still believes he is.
Appearance is everything to him. He's always immaculately

dressed in something from his expensive – but still tasteful – wardrobe. His personal barber is always in the house, making sure his hair is cut and then dyed back to the jet black of his youth. And he still treats his body, his health, like an athlete. He'll never say no to a steak in Cameron's, or a slab of ribs in the back yard, but the house is full of fresh fruit and vegetables. I've heard him make the same joke dozens of times over the years: 'Yeah, I went to the doctor's for a check-up the other day. I dunno, he said there's something unusual going on with my body … I'm ageing twenty years younger than I should be!'

And then he'd break into that unmistakable laugh of his. He would never use his health as an excuse, unless he was bedridden with no other option, and that's what has me worried. I call him.

'Emanuel, what's going on? Are you OK? How come you're not doing the fight?'

'Yeah, I'm just not feeling well. I have to go in and get a couple of tests done but they don't think it's a big deal. I'm not really sure what's wrong but it's nothing too serious anyway.'

There are a thousand other things that he'd rather talk about, so it doesn't take long to change the subject. But the following day, Perry calls me from Chicago.

'I don't know if you've been speaking to Emanuel at all lately, but he's in a pretty bad way. You should call him when you have a chance and see what's up.'

He's in hospital when I get through to him, and he tries to brush me off again.

'They're doing some tests now. It's not going to be a big deal. I'll be fine in a few weeks, don't worry.'

I've spent too much time with him, heard him tell enough white lies, to know when he's not being completely truthful. I can hear it in the intonation of his voice. Something's not right. When I get off the phone, I book a flight, and I'm in Detroit by the following afternoon.

Sugar Hill's mam, Laverne, is there waiting for me at the airport to pick me up, and as she drives me to the hospital and fills me in on the last few days, it becomes clear that this is not as trivial as Emanuel wants me to believe. Whatever is wrong with him, and nobody seems fully sure, the doctors are taking it very seriously.

When we get to his room, Emanuel is awake, sitting up, communicating. But he looks his age, which is not something I ever would have said before. The machines at his bedside buzz and beep and whirr. The start of a smile forms on his face when he sees me come through the door. His hair is grey. I noticed that he hadn't dyed it when he flew down to El Paso, but it's even more pronounced now. There's a tiredness to his face. When he speaks to me, I can hear it in his voice.

There's a lot of idle talk, dancing around the subject like we would across the ring. I catch a few snippets as the doctors and nurses come in to check that Emanuel is comfortable, make a few notes, a slight adjustment here and there. Whatever they're running those tests for, it doesn't sound like something that has been just diagnosed. This is something that he's had for a while.

Nobody says it directly, but it reveals itself gradually and then all at once. He has cancer.

I think Emanuel knew it himself the night of the Chávez fight. He flew back to Detroit afterwards with Maud and my mam and my dad, and whatever way he had parted with Maud, there was an air of resignation, an acceptance that he had taken me as far as he could on this journey. It all made sense now. He may have known for a long time that the odds were stacked against him, but he would never admit that to himself, or burden anyone close to him with the worry. It wouldn't be at all out of character for him to put his head down and carry on living his life as if nothing out of the ordinary was happening. There were plenty of occasions over the years when I saw him have blazing rows, deliver words that hit like punches, and then the very next day, sweep the argument away and hug it out like nothing had ever happened. That was his way of dealing with difficult situations.

I sleep in the hospital that night, and the next night as well. There's a little bunk beside Emanuel's bed that I'm able to pull down and use. I could get a lift back to the house, or stay in Sugar Hill's, but all of the time that we've spent together over the last six years now seems like nowhere near enough, so I stay. If he wakes up and needs anything, I'll be there.

I've been with him in Detroit for a couple of days when the doctors tell him that he needs to be transferred to a hospital in Chicago. A specialist facility for cancer treatment. He asks me to go with him in the air ambulance. In a room full of immediate family – his wife, his daughters, his sister – I'm suddenly very conscious that I am not. But they know our relationship, our bond, how close we are. If that is Emanuel's wish, if that's what will make him comfortable when he's being transferred, that's what they want too. He insists.

'Andy is coming with me. I want Andy to fly with me.'

When we get to Chicago, I stay there with him again, asking the doctors the kind of questions that I think might be helpful, about his treatment plan, his progress, the timeline for his recovery. One of them gently, indirectly, guides my train of thought in a different direction that I haven't been able to bring myself to fully consider. Emanuel's illness is the kind that needs to be cared for rather than treated. He will get everything he needs to make sure that he's comfortable, but it's highly unlikely that he will ever get to leave.

For those few days, we do our best to live life as normal – as normal as is possible within the sterile confines of a hospital room. We watch Martínez v Chávez on a laptop together, and even now, we're barely able to bring ourselves to relive that night in June. Still too raw. I'm there beside him when Wladimir rings from camp to see how Emanuel is doing, when he'll be able to fly out to Austria. And I watch as Emanuel palms off his concern in the exact same way that he had done to me only a few days earlier.

'It's nothing. It's just a few tests. You keep training. I'll be out of here in a while. You've got Johnathon there with you. Keep doing what you're doing. I'll be over soon.'

I sit there, and I can't help thinking: you won't. But right up until the very end, he wouldn't give in. He kept that same steely resolve, whether that was for his own benefit or for ours.

The morning comes for me to leave and fly back to London, but I have no intention of going anywhere. I booked my flights for a five-day visit, hoping for a quick trip to say hello, catch up, and reassure myself that everything was as innocuous as he was promising. Now that I'm here, now that I know the reality of it, I don't want to leave.

I tell Emanuel that I've a flight booked, but I'm going to change it and stay with him for a few more days. We've flown together on so many occasions, I should be able to anticipate his response. I've never known a man so particular about airports and flying, totting up his air miles with a book-keeper's precision. An encyclopaedic knowledge of every terminal in America: check-in desk to the left, wait until we go through security, the shops are better on the far side, here for this type of food, there for that type. All of the staff seem to know him, and he knows them too, his $20 bills out and ready to go, the secret handshake that inevitably saw us rushed to the top of the queue no matter what. He would never let me miss a flight.

'Andy, go and catch your flight home. I'll see you soon.'

I know leaving the hospital that day that I will never see him again, and I leave anyway. It's what he wanted. There's not a day goes by that I don't think about him. I call him, send him messages for as long as I can, and after that, I keep in touch with his family for weeks. I see the first reports, the first tributes, the first obituaries, and I fear the worst. Diane, his sister, assures me that they've got it wrong. He's still there, still hanging in, fighting until the last.

< >

The bell rings through the Greater Grace Temple, one of boxing's most beautiful traditions. We stand, and Emanuel receives his final ten count.

Aretha Franklin sings from the pulpit, a tribute to her friend. Tommy Hearns promises to be stoic, to be strong, but the tears come anyway. Sugar Ray, Wladimir, Lewis, Holyfield, they're all there to tell their stories, share their memories of a great man and a great life.

When it's my turn, I stand and I tell them about the Emanuel I knew. I have some words prepared on a page in front of me in case I need them, but even in sadness, they come easy. I speak from the heart. I loved him.

I'll always be grateful to Emanuel. He let me live in his house and live a dream.

He'll always be in my heart.

He was such a permanent presence in my life. More than a mentor. A second father figure. It's impossible to come to terms with the fact that he is gone. That he'll never shout across the hall again to tell me the crazy story of whatever had just happened on his most recent phone call. That he'll never see me become a world champion.

In my grief, I find strength. This man gave me everything, and I was there with him, for him, when he needed me the most. I got to see him, care for him, spend that precious time with him. He knew I was there, appreciated that I had come. I can't bear to think of the alternative, that after seven years living under his roof, I might have received a short phone call in London one day to tell me that he was gone. No time to say goodbye. No time to show him how deeply I cared. The guilt would have ruined me.

The Chávez fight, how I let them play me, rob me, it haunts me. I'm not willing to be old and grey and go to my grave with that being the day that my dream died. I've given too much of myself to allow that. I'm only twenty-eight, still good enough to win a world title, still young enough. I'm not finished. I could go back to the Kronk and try to build towards another shot, but I need something fresh, something new. It takes me a while to confront the thought, to accept that it might be time for me to leave Detroit.

I don't have a shortlist of coaches that I'm interested in speaking to; Adam Booth is the only one. I don't know Adam, have never met him, only watched his work from a distance. He doesn't train too many fighters, but when he does, he turns them into champions. He made his name with David Haye, took him from a teenager all the way through to world champion at cruiserweight, and then up a division to win a heavyweight world title as well. He seems to be on the cusp of something really special with George Groves as well, and that has impressed me more than anything. Emanuel didn't like him, formed a first impression of him as this brash, cocky Londoner when Wladimir fought against Haye, and it stuck. The T-shirts, the YouTube videos, he found it all a bit cheap and disrespectful. The truth is, he might have felt a little bit threatened: a younger man, well-spoken, a good coach with a good fighter.

I call down to meet him in his gym in Vauxhall, and I'm straight in at the deep end. Adam knows why I'm here, and now we quickly need to figure out if we're wasting our time or not. He grabs me some gym gear, tells me to get changed, and puts on the pads. I get loose, light, and I'm ready to go. He holds his arm out, calls the shot, and I freeze. I've done padwork thousands of times and it's always the same: you hear the shot and react on instinct. But I can't do what Adam is asking me. The footwork, the headwork that's required, it's something totally unfamiliar. It's simple, basic stuff but my mind can't parse it. We slow it down and Adam walks me through it.

'If I call breakout, this is what I want you to do. You need to take that lead right foot and step it outside me. Get low, bring your left shoulder down towards your knee, and while you're in that crouch, transfer all of your weight onto that outside leg and pivot around to the outside.'

Take me back to Detroit, to the Kronk, to the heat. I know how to box. A few months ago I fought for a world title, and yet this feels so alien, so unnatural. I don't understand. Adam is patient. Come down to the gym when you can, he tells me. See how we do things around here, see how you go over the next couple of weeks. Then you can make a decision.

I want to believe that a world title is there on the horizon, that I just have to reach out and grab it. I convince myself that the gap that separates contenders and champions is a small one, that it would only take a few tweaks to bridge that distance. A couple of weeks with Adam is enough to expose that as pure fantasy. It's hard, hard work. I'm not fit enough to do the moves that Adam wants me to learn. I've never developed those muscles. I'm drained physically by the time we finish our sessions. Technically, the demands are just as severe. I've grown up as a Kronk boxer, it is who I am, and every instinct under pressure is to go back to what I already know. Starting from scratch, with a blank canvas, would be so much easier. Instead, Adam has to erase the old patterns in my mind, wipe the muscle memory clean, before he can teach me in his way. That's the only way to do it, and it can't happen overnight.

Emanuel always said that there are coaches and trainers in boxing, but very few teachers. He was a teacher and Adam is a teacher. A teacher can break down and articulate the moves and the techniques, but also the fighters and the styles. They can communicate clearly. They're respected, without commanding or demanding it, and that respect is a two-way street. You have to buy in 100 per cent to what they're telling you because the moment you have a doubt about a coach, the moment you feel that what he's telling you is not the best strategy, the number one option, the optimum approach for you, the moment that he has anything but the entirety of your respect and admiration, he's lost you. As a fighter, you have to have blind faith. With Zaur, Billy, Emanuel, and now Adam, I always did.

It takes a long time for me to adjust to Adam, and Adam to me, but after Emanuel's death, there is no place else I wanted to be. My contract with the investors in Chicago had run out. I had verbally said that I would renew, but if I'm moving to Adam, everything needs a fresh start. It's the only way he'll agree to take me on.

'Look, if we're going to do this fully, I have to have complete control. If you want to be able to train here, I'm going to have to manage you because I need to be able to make the calls that need to be made without anyone else interfering.'

The phone calls start again. Perry rings, leaves me messages: Andy, call me, I'm very disappointed, we need to talk. After the calls, it's the legal letters. They argue that the eight months I spent out injured when I had the surgery to fix my cut was time owed to them, that I'm still under contract until they've been compensated for that lost time. They request that we take the dispute to arbitration. The legal advice I get is simple and clear: go to arbitration and explain what happened. That's exactly what I do. In the end, I just want it to go away so that I can go back to concentrating on my boxing. I settle out of court and pay them $25,000.

There were times over the years when I didn't always see eye to eye with the Chicago group, when our relationship was complicated, messy even, but that's boxing. When you strip it all away, I would never have even got this far without their support and investment. Perry, in particular, was always very good to me. Money was no object. He flew me all over the world to make sure I could train with the best of the best. He never said no to anything that Emanuel wanted for me. He made sure that I had everything I needed to get to the top. Without their support, I could never have turned pro in the first place. My life would be completely different. It's disappointing to end on a disagreement, but when all is said and done, I'm grateful for all they've done for me. My mind is made up: if I'm basing myself in London, I need to go my own way.

The only way to test what I'm learning with Adam is in the ring. We take a fight in Belfast against Anthony Fitzgerald on Carl Frampton's undercard in February 2013. Everything is new again. We don't have a pre-fight routine, we don't have a way that we do things. I have my way and Adam has his, and we're going through this together for the very first time. You discuss things, try to plan and figure out what will work best, but you can't prepare for it until you go through it. The dressing room, the walk to the ring, the corner: nothing is the same.

It's my debut except this time it's different. That first night in Detroit, I didn't know any other way of doing things. I was nervous but I knew it was a fight that I would win. I can't say the same for Fitzgerald. He's a tough guy and he'll bring a huge crowd up the road with him from Dublin. All the pressure is on me. Back in a place where people know me. Where people expect things of me.

I block out those concerns and think about what we've discussed, how I want to fight tonight and what I want to achieve. Adam stands as he wraps my hands. I miss Emanuel. He'll always be on my mind, in every dressing room, for the rest of my career. But I can't become a prisoner of the past. There are no world titles there; there can be in my future.

W hen you start out in life, when you're young, you
have dreams. You look thirty or forty years down
the road and project. You imagine the things
that you will achieve, the type of person that you will be and
the life you will live. Everybody's dreams are different,
weighted towards a different purpose. Some people dream
of fame and fortune; some people dream of family and
friends. And those dreams, the possibility that they might
someday come true, they make you happy.

In time, as you grow up, your dreams move from
tomorrow to today. They stop being ambitions that exist in
the distant future and become a lot more present, more
urgent; they will either happen in the here and now, or never.
And if they don't happen, if your dreams don't materialise in
the way that you once hoped, you slowly have to accept that
you didn't make it. You settle into the life that you do have
and make peace with it, live out the rest of it with the
knowledge that you didn't make it. Live with the thoughts of
what might have been. It's easy to do if your dreams never
meant that much to you, if they were just idle thoughts
that once seemed nice. But the more stock you once placed
in your dreams, the harder it is to live with their failure to
come true.

It's a tough realisation to come to. The sinking feeling.
The thoughts of what you could have done or should have
done. The regret. It builds day by day. I have a lot of time to
think, lying alone in this small room. A bed, a desk, and no
more. The sound of strangers opening and closing the front

door as they come and go punctuates the loneliness. I think about Detroit, Emanuel, and how I've gone from a world where boxing was everything to one where it is a complete irrelevance, where nobody cares if I'm a boxer because nobody even knows my name. It wasn't perfect but it was better than this crushing aimlessness, with more than just a feeling that you've been forgotten. The certainty, it destroys you.

When I first left Detroit, I moved my entire life into the bedroom that Maud was renting in Finsbury Park. I arrived without much warning, temporarily, but their house of five soon became a house of six. I lived there with Maud and four of her female friends for a while, getting the Tube to the gym in Vauxhall in the morning and back again in the evening. But Maud moved home to Dublin for work at around the same time that Adam moved his base to a new gym in Purley in Surrey. I needed somewhere to stay, somewhere that didn't involve traversing the length of London every day, which is how I ended up in this house. This room. I eat here, I read a book or watch a few episodes of some series on my laptop, and I sleep. Apart from the gym, this room is my world.

There are five of us in the house, I think, living in virtual anonymity. We share a kitchen and we share the bathroom, and we still manage to completely avoid each other. It's almost impressive. We pass once or twice in the hallway and say hello. Somebody might come into the kitchen and start getting ready to make their dinner just as I'm washing up. But that's about it. I live here for five or six months, and at the end of it all, these people are as much strangers to me as they were at the beginning.

Most weekends, I stay with my dad to have some company. There's a saying that at the end of every man's journey, he ends up back at the beginning with new perspective; I never thought it would be so literal as to lead me back to a site in London. I've been away for so long and it's great to catch up, to spend time with my dad, and with Roger and Hayley who live in Romford too. I arrive in my ten-year-old Vauxhall Zafira and park up beside the brand-new Mercs and Golfs and BMWs that belong to the young gypsy lads who have already been out working for a couple of years. Gypsy culture, it's all about what you have, and I'm supposed to be the superstar with loads of money, the boxer who was on all of these big cards in America, the man who fought for a world title. People think that I'm a role model, someone to look up to, someone to aspire to be like, but that's not the reality of my life. That's not how I feel. All I feel is inadequate.

This so-called celebrity is a trap. Even if I packed it all in tomorrow, walked away and quit, I can't go and work. I can't go and get a job. I can't go to work on a building site. Oh look, there's Andy Lee, cutting my trees and hedges. He's the guy that fought Chávez for a world title there last year. If you do that, you're admitting defeat. You have to be prepared for the whole world to see you through that lens, the failed boxer, the shoulda woulda coulda guy, for the rest of your life. You have to be ready to live with that regret forever.

I can't give up. I look at Adam with his nice house, his nice car, and his wonderful family, the security and the happiness that he has, and I see everything that I could ever want in life. Boxing is the only thing that can give me that, the only way that I can provide for myself and my family. And I will have a family soon. When I asked Maud to marry me, and she said yes, it was the happiest day of my life. She would never expect anything of me. She would never want me to feel this pressure I'm feeling. But I can't outgrow that feeling that binds up a man's worth with his ability to provide a house, a home, even a caravan for his family. I can't do those things for Maud, and it eats away at me.

We get married in the south of France in the summer of 2013, a few weeks after I knock Darryl Cunningham out in New York. We look at houses in Dublin but every meeting with bank managers and mortgage brokers ends with a variation of the same response: we couldn't give that kind of money to a boxer and a musician. And with every no, the bleak reality of this situation that I'm in hits home again. I have some money saved, but life is long, and there are no guarantees about jobs or income or any real prospects in my future. There's no monthly living allowance since I broke the deal with the Chicago group, so every penny I spend now – rent, travel, food – is coming directly out of my savings, a bet hedged against the only financial guarantee I have to last me for the rest of my life.

I'm living from week to week. I go to Tesco and start counting up the loose change in my pocket: £15 one week, £24 the next; just about enough for the shopping.

Logic becomes warped, and everything I've done becomes an opportunity for regret and recrimination. Myself and Maud have had fantastic lives since we've met each other, enjoyed the journey, experienced the world, but what good is all of that to me now? What good are those memories? All of those many happy times, they're not going to buy us a house or make ends meet now.

In my most optimistic moments, I convince myself that I'm only two wins away from having it all, that one fight, one win against a ranked fighter would whip me out of the wilderness and put me right back in the mix for a title shot. But the scars of the Chávez fight have never fully healed. After all of this, even if I get myself back into a position for a big fight, there's no guarantee that I won't get screwed over again. There are times when I want to give up. I'll live with the consequences. I tell Adam exactly how I feel.

'What is the point in all of this? Seriously. What's the point?'

Two wins away, maybe, but I can't even get a fight. My confidence, my self-esteem, it's all in tatters. It feels like I've been abandoned, cut loose, and left to find my own way out of this mess. Nobody wants to know. Adam has other fighters to look after too, other priorities. DiBella Entertainment are still my promoter, but my contract with them is only for two fights a year and they've already taken care of that much. Damian tries everything, constantly on the phone, canvassing, trying to get me the right opponent, and then any opponent at all. I'm booked for the Fury–Haye undercard in September but that's cancelled. Six months go by and there's still nothing. Nothing until a Tuesday night in November when Adam rings me at home.

'There's a space on the card on Saturday night. Do you want it?'

'Yeah, give me the fight, I'll take it.'

I'm only getting over a bit of an illness but I'm not even thinking about that. Put me in. My opponent, Ferenc Hafner, is barely better than a journeyman. I put him down in the first, and twice more in the second. It's not the kind of win that's going to solve any of my problems. It's not going to turn any heads or pay many bills. For tonight, none of that matters. I'm just glad to be back boxing again.

<figure>‹ ›</figure>

Adam has the callipers out, tugging at skin folds, checking my body fat, sizing me up. No good conversation ever started with the words, 'Come over here and let me check your weight'. I'm instantly sceptical of his motives and, as it happens, I'm right to be. It's more than just a quick hop up on the scales; I've had physicals that are less thorough.

'What's going on? What are you checking for?'

'You know, I think you could make light-middleweight.'

My bemused look says it all. I was fighting at 165lbs when I was a scraggly, scrawny teenager. I've been fighting consistently at 160, give or take a pound or two, for pretty much my entire professional career. Even the suggestion that I could do 154, that I might possibly be carrying around another six spare pounds that I could afford to shed and still hop into the ring fighting fit, it sounds like lunacy. He's insistent. The numbers, the measurements, they add up. He makes me talk him through my weekly meal plan, and nothing that I'm saying is doing anything to discourage him.

'You'll do it, you'll make light-middleweight. We'll need to make a few small changes, but I'm confident that you will if you follow what I say. It's there on you.'

It will be tough, but it's a shot to nothing. If I can't do it, I'll keep going at middleweight and hope for a breakthrough. But I can see the logic to Adam's plan. There are a lot of good fights out there at light-middleweight, good opponents that will get me back in primetime TV slots, get people excited and talking about me again. Remind people that I exist.

Adam rings Lou DiBella, tells him that I'm dropping down a division, and that we're looking for fights at 154. I've nothing left to lose.

For the first year that we worked together, there was definitely a bit of distance between me and Adam. There were a lot of times when he wasn't in the gym and I was training instead with his assistants, Gary Logan and Darren Chan. It was Darren, along with Roger and Joey Gamache, who did the corner for my fight against Cunningham in New York, not Adam. It took a while before he really became invested in me. If I had turned around and told him that I was walking away, he couldn't have argued. It was only after his split from George Groves that we got to know each other better. I could see how hurt he was by it. He had been working with George since he turned pro, mentored him all the way to a world title shot, and then they split up just before the fight. Adam had only really trained David Haye and George until I came along, and he had never experienced anything like it. I'd seen it happen a million times before: the disillusionment that sets in when such a close relationship breaks down. We spoke about it a few times and became good friends through it.

I learned a lot watching George in that first year, how hard he was working, the level of training that Adam demanded of him, and the extra work he was expected to put in outside the ring. A great sparring partner to have and a lovely guy too. It was a shame to see him go, but when he did, it opened up a huge opportunity for me. George was Adam's biggest fighter, with everything pointing towards the Carl Froch fight, and I was being squeezed to the side a bit. When George left, Adam had a lot more time to work with me.

Richard Towers, another fighter in the gym, became a good friend as well, and the three of us formed a close band.

Adam trains his fighters to have a very athletic style based on reflexes and power and speed. He puts me through an insane amount of physical conditioning. We start at 11am, and the morning session takes however long it takes. Monday is a heavy day, Tuesday is more technical work, and then I have a day off on Wednesday before coming back for sparring on a Thursday. We call Friday 'Fuck 'Em Up Friday'. Pretty self-explanatory, really: fifteen intense rounds, a different exercise in every round. The evening sessions are reserved for a mixture of short and long runs on the road to build up my endurance, and some speed work on the track. Fuck 'Em Up Friday finishes with treadmill sprints: twenty reps at a minimum speed of 20kph, twenty seconds on, ten seconds off, non-stop for ten minutes. If I get through that without throwing up, which is no guarantee, we increase the speed or increase the reps, and then the final step is to increases the incline on the machine. I'm back in the gym on Saturday morning for more weights, more strength work.

In any sport, you have to master the basics, the fundamentals, before you grasp the essence of it. The Kronk style of fighting was all about staying tall with straight legs, evading punches by leaning back and leaning out of range. Adam wants me to sit into my legs, bend my knees, move my head to make my opponent miss, duck low, and roll under their punches. I understand what he's trying to teach me but it doesn't come as second nature. I'm guessing. I watch him training other fighters and try to emulate them in the ring and in spars, but I don't know how to do it instinctively. Everything is very deliberate; I have to think about it seriously to make it happen. Boxing really is all about repetition.

Adam is obsessive, all-consumed by boxing. He'll lie in bed in the morning thinking about it, why something was done in a certain way, how it can be improved, and then when you meet him, he'll give you the new gospel for the day. Gospel is the only word for it because he inspires this intense devotion to his way of doing things – the lifestyle, the mindset, the attitude, the approach. He is so committed, so resolute in what he says, that you totally believe everything he tells you. He has a magnetism about him. I see how everyone around him looks after themselves, how they get a kick out of eating clean and living a healthy life. Those gorgeous ribs in Vicky's, the big steaks in Cameron's, they're all off the menu now.

I eventually become a fighter in Adam's style, but what he teaches me isn't always the best thing for me to do in a given moment. There are times when I have to go back to being the Kronk fighter, when things aren't going well in spars and in fights and I have to draw on the skills that I learned from Emanuel and from Sugar Hill. They still work too. A lot of coaches want it to be their way or the highway, but Adam understands that there's a lot that he can learn from me, from my experience, as well. He's open to it. He starts to use cocoa butter instead of Vaseline on his fighters' faces. He starts to sit down when he's wrapping their hands.

Adam books me a fight on a card in Esbjerg, a seaside town in Denmark, in April 2014. He pays the purse himself for my opponent, Frank Haroche Horta, an average French fighter. No kind of pedigree to suggest that he'll give me any trouble but that's not the priority. He's available and he can make light-middleweight so he fits the bill.

Now every mouthful of food, every sip of water, everything is measured and monitored with a new precision. The kitchen becomes a lab of cups and half-cups, teaspoons and tablespoons. No margin for error. I'm allowed two egg whites for breakfast, maybe three – but no yolks – a single piece of Ryvita with a rub of vegetarian spread so thin it's hardly there, and a cup of tea. That's it for the morning. After our morning training session, I have a big bowl of porridge made with water – no milk – and either sultanas or raisins. I try to have a nap in the afternoon, an hour or two of recovery, and when I wake up, I can have a piece of fruit: an apple or a banana. When I get back from our evening training session, I cook my dinner: a small piece of fish or chicken with some veg and some grains on the side. Once a week, for a treat, I swap in a little bit of red meat: a small, lean steak. The ritual, the boredom of sticking religiously to pretty much the exact same food in the exact same quantities at the exact same time every day, that's as tough as anything. I persevere and it becomes habit, one less thing to think about most days. Once I can see the weight start to come down, once I know it's working, it gets easier.

I fly out to Denmark a few days before the fight with Bobby Rich, the strength and conditioning coach that Adam uses for all of his fighters. Bobby puts me through my paces, trying to get the weight off without sacrificing my strength and my power. By the day of the weigh-in, I'm down at 156lbs, two pounds over what I would need to be for a title fight at light-middleweight but close enough on this occasion. Job done. After months of trying to decide whether a half-cup of sweet potato means four cubes or five, I've convinced myself that I'm allowed a celebration. Getting down to the weight was the real target; the fight should look after itself. I go to the cinema that afternoon, but when I get there, I'm dying to eat something stupid. I buy myself a bag of M&Ms and a Magnum and make sure that I enjoy them.

It's only much later that evening that I discover how monumentally bad an idea that was. The shooting, stabbing pains wake me up in the middle of the night. I'm in agony with stomach cramps. I go into the bathroom and sit on the toilet, half-asleep, to see if that will help. Nothing happens. I go back to bed and try to sleep it off, hoping that it will be OK in the morning, praying that it's not food poisoning or a vomiting bug or anything that might stop me from fighting. Every time I start to doze off, an invisible hand grabs a hold of the knot in my stomach and twists it. I go back to the toilet again. I could wait there all night; it won't do any good. The cramps have eased a bit by the next morning but even a few pre-fight jitters don't do much to help things along the next day; there wouldn't be room in there for the butterflies anyway. In the end, I don't hang around for too long after I beat Horta. Once business is taken care of in the ring, I've business to attend to elsewhere.

The fight itself is much tougher than I expected. He celebrates like he's won it at the end. His trainer is nearly in there with us before the final bell goes, lifting him and carrying him around the ring. I've no doubts about the result but he's a gutsy fighter, and when I ease off towards the end, he's good enough to take advantage and pick off a couple of rounds. I win two cards by a point, and we're level on the third one. Not exactly an exclamation point against this calibre of opponent but a majority decision makes it sound a lot closer than it ever was.

From the moment I beat Horta, I'm barely out of Adam's sight. He invites me to come and live with him and his family. He knows how I'm living, bouncing from room to room on short-term leases, going back up to Romford or flying home to Ireland at the weekend, and then back to the same depressing four walls on a Monday. It can't be good for my mental health, and even if that kind of environment isn't holding me back, there's no way that it's helping to make me better. He can see how disciplined I am with my food and my diet, how hard I'm pushing myself in the gym and on the track, maxing out in every little session. When we train, I'm the leader, bringing that Kronk spirit to south London, setting the standards, driving everybody around me to be better so that they drive me to be better. I'm in the shape of my life, leaner, more defined, than ever before.

The Booths' house becomes a home away from home. His wife, Claire, his daughters, his dog, they are all like family to me. They do everything they can to make me feel welcome and help me settle in. The worry of having to dip into our savings to rent a grim box is gone. Overnight, another nagging weight disappears. Living with Adam becomes a replica of all of the best parts of the relationship I had with Emanuel. He makes sure I'm eating right, sleeping right, that I always have a bottle of water in my hand that I can sip on. It copper-fastens our understanding of one another. We might have started out as coach and boxer, but that changes with time. Adam becomes one of my closest friends, someone whose advice I rely on, someone who I would trust with my life.

‹ ›

My right hook is my killer punch. When I throw it, when I feel that power, it's addictive.

It starts in the hips, as if you're swinging a golf club or a baseball bat, and then your torso pulls through and the rest of your body follows. Your elbow and your forearm run parallel to the ground, with the line of your clenched knuckles perpendicular to the floor and the bend of your thumb pointing up at the ceiling. If you come down on the punch from above, or pull up on it from below, you lose some of the power. It all happens in one fluid motion, each element connected, coordinated, without even thinking: hip, torso, shoulder, fist.

Conventionally, a boxer fights with his weaker hand as his lead hand, so you would expect a southpaw like me to have a strong left hand and a weaker right. My right hand has always been my strong hand though. I write with my right hand; I kick a football with my right foot. I only started boxing as a southpaw because that's how Ned shaped up. He's right-handed too, and as a kid, he fought in an orthodox stance with a left-hand lead. One summer he broke his left hand but kept going to the gym and started training with his right instead. When the cast eventually came off, he stayed boxing as a southpaw, and he passed it on to me and Roger when we started to learn from him. When I started to take boxing seriously, around the age of eleven or twelve, I quickly realised that my left hand was terrible. I couldn't really throw a good uppercut or left hook from a southpaw stance. I developed it over the years but my right hand has always been far stronger. It's unusual, but some of the best fighters in the world box with their stronger hand as their lead. Oscar De La Hoya is a left-handed fighter who stays in the orthodox stance, and so is Miguel Cotto. It makes sense, even if it goes against the norm. Ninety per cent of your work in the ring is done with your lead hand – jabbing, hooking, setting up your next shot – so there's an argument to use your strong hand and get the most out of it.

The right hook has always been my best weapon but it's changed over the years, evolved at different points and in different circumstances. In my amateur days, it was more of a side-step. I'd catch my opponent with the punch and slip out from underneath them all at once. When I started working with Emanuel, it was a quick punch, snapped in – a surprising shot that hurt people because they never saw it coming. Under Sugar Hill, it took on more of a muscular strength. He emphasised power punching, hitting hard, using your lead hand to control the opponent and control the distance between you. When he was training me, my right hook would start from the same tall stance that Emanuel always taught, but it was drilled in with a bit more venom. When I move to London with Adam, he adds the final touches. He gets me to sit low in my legs and spring up out of a squat position, which generates even more power. It's not just my arm throwing the punch anymore, it's my whole body, the momentum starting from my feet and rising all the way up through my fist.

I rarely throw a right hook as a lead or as a standalone punch. I throw it as a counter-punch, which is where it really comes into its own as a lethal weapon. That's why it has been so successful for me. Most boxers are orthodox fighters, favouring a right-hand lead, but when they throw their punch, instead of stepping away to make them miss, I'll take the chance and step in and trade with them at the same time. I might get hit myself, but in doing so I might also force open this small window of opportunity where I can do some real damage. Instinctively, when they throw their right, they draw their left hand back in towards them. They're focused on the punch that they're throwing, not even suspecting that one is coming in return. If you time it right, it leaves this gap for you to connect. It turns their own momentum, their own power, back on them with double the impact. It's a beautiful thing.

I believe in the punch. There's great trust there. Even if I fall behind in the first half of a fight, I know that I have a chance. I know that I'll always have opportunities. A lot of my highlight reel knockouts are sweet right hooks. Because of that, people start to see me as a puncher, biding my time, waiting for this one big shot. They think it's all I've got. I play it up when I'm asked about it in interviews or when my opponent calls me out as a one-punch boxer. I tell them that they're right, that I have this big hook, that I'm going to throw it, and warn them that if it connects, it's lights out. It suits me if they're obsessing over one punch. It means that they're not concentrating on any of my other weapons, and no matter what people say, I know I have plenty.

Besides, when it finds its mark and connects properly, it won't matter in the slightest how many times they've watched it on tape. My right hook is a gift.

<＜ ＞>

Opponents like John Jackson are the reason why I dropped down to light-middleweight. This is no undercard filler; it's the real deal. He's 18–1, four years younger than me, not at world level yet, but certainly moving in the right direction. Ranked fourth in the division. Of royal blood, too. His dad Julian had a reputation as the hardest puncher in the world in his day, lights out if he so much as looked at you with his right hand, his calling card. Junior's picking up a bit of a buzz himself, not just trading off the family name. They say he's got the old man's power. I'm about to find out.

We're under no illusions. This is Madison Square Garden, not B.B. King's. My first serious fight in two years, since Chávez, since moving to join Adam. Our first time in the furnace as a team, the first true test of our partnership, fly or fall. I might have been forgotten, but I'm not gone yet. There's curiosity and intrigue there when the build-up gets going. Everything is up for discussion: the move to Adam, the drop in weight, the standstill that my career has been at.

It's set as my true light-middleweight debut. No couple of pounds' leeway; no M&Ms and Magnums. Physically, it's absolutely gruelling. I'm tipping about 160 when we get to New York at the start of fight week, right on track. As soon as I get out of bed, I'm into all of my sweat gear and onto the treadmill for twenty minutes. I do it for a second morning, but it doesn't seem to be making any difference, the weight is not coming off. Adam is totally puzzled:

'What are you wearing? What layers do you have on?'

'I'm wearing all of it. I've got my T-shirt on and then all the sweat gear on top of it.'

'No, you've got to take the T-shirt off. That's what's stopping the weight from coming down.'

I do as he says, put the sweat gear directly onto my skin, and then put all of my jumpers and T-shirts on top before I get back on the treadmill to go again. It starts to work immediately.

My digestive system is so disrupted by the weight cut that I can't go to the bathroom. I try perching on the toilet bowl and squatting down over it to force myself to go because I've read somewhere that it's a more natural, evolutionary way to get your bowels moving. I look ridiculous, and it doesn't help. I spend the last hour before the weigh-in sprinting up and down the corridor outside my room in the Affinia Hotel. I get on the scales for the last time, and I'm still over by 0.1lbs. Adam tells me it's time to go.

'Don't worry, that last bit will come off. It's hot outside. You'll lose that much on the walk across the road.'

Adam's right. I make the weight, bang on the 154lb limit. As soon as I'm off the scales, all I want to do is eat and drink, but I learned that lesson the hard way the last time, and my body is even weaker now. I get dressed and Adam passes me over the small Tupperware container of boiled rice that we made earlier. Just rice, and a small bit of salt. It takes all of my discipline not to shovel it into me. I sit there, in the back room of the arena, and graze. Tiny little bites, picking at a couple of grains at a time, chewing each one thoroughly. I've brought a drink too, some water, and something isotonic. It's been days since I've had anything other than a couple of sips of water. I've been pumping sweat all morning. My tongue is stuck to my mouth and my skin feels like paper, like it would tear at the slightest touch. Adam hands it to me and my body turns into a hyperactive college kid at a frat party, screaming at me to chug chug chug. I block it out and take a sip, and then another one, careful not to rehydrate too quickly.

Life goes in slow motion for the next half-hour. Once I've reintroduced my body to the forgotten concept of food and liquids, I can think about eating something that resembles a conventional meal. Nothing fancy, chicken and pasta, salmon and pasta, whatever we can get nearby. Finding somewhere near the hotel is important as well because after about half a plate I'm so full, using so much energy on this unfamiliar process of digesting food, that I'm hardly able to walk. By later that night, I'll be ready to attempt another meal. The next day is all about getting the balancing act right, rehydrating and replenishing, putting as much of that lost weight back on as you can without overdoing it and harming your performance. At middleweight, I usually put on about twelve pounds; this time, I manage about eight or nine by the time we get to the dressing room.

Mentally, those final days are a constant denial. It's more than just the starvation and the dehydration. I'm training hard at the same time, mining my lifeless body for energy that it doesn't have and doesn't want to give so that I can burn off a couple more ounces and get closer to the target. I lie in bed, thinking about how hungry I am, how thirsty I am. In the more dangerous moments, I let my mind wander to what I'm going to eat when this is all over. It's draining, it's exhausting, but I try to harness it, let it embolden me. When I step into the ring, I remind myself of the pain, the sacrifice that I've just forced myself through. I did it so that I can fight. I'm not going to let this fella beat me after I've starved myself for three or four weeks. I'm not going to let this fella beat me after I've only been allowed to sip water, after I couldn't so much as go to the toilet. No chance. I haven't put myself through that torture to come and lose. I remind myself of that. I'm going to win this fight.

Back in the Garden for the first time since I stopped the city. Seven years ago now. That Daniels fight was one of the big crossroads in the early part of my career, the springboard to bigger and better things. Now I'm back at the same crossroads again and the signs are stark in their simplicity: one says make, the other says break.

Dropping down a division, the obvious risk is that you become a bit weaker. Even if you manage to preserve the power and strength in the punches that you're doling out, your body is that little bit less robust when it comes to absorbing them. When Jackson hits me with his best shot, two minutes into the first round, everything becomes involuntary. I'm off balance and I'm unsighted. I make the first move, throw a left hook, but he ducks underneath it and my arm clips the top of his head. His counter, a right over the top, arrives before I even know it's coming. Bang. I'm on the floor.

I've seen the ring from every angle except this one. In thirty-four fights nobody has ever knocked me down. Not Vera, not Chávez, nobody. I commit so fully to my own punch that my left leg crumples as soon as his lands. I'm hurt but I'm back on my feet by the time the referee picks up the count at four. I take my time, stand still, and look him in the eye. Five. Compose myself. Six. A deep breath. Seven. I raise my gloves and nod at him. I'm OK.

Jackson corners me with impetuous haste, ready to end me there and then. He drops his hands, thinking only of his finish, and I sting him with a left hook. Enough to make him think again. Enough to weather the storm and get me to the bell. In the corner, I reassure myself. There's still a long, long way to go. Nine more rounds. Get it together. Box your way back in. You'll be fine.

It's a good fight. Dramatic, entertaining, lots of action. Which makes it more of a pity that he's winning practically all of these early rounds as they tick by. He catches me again in the fourth with one of his dad's punches, a hard right lead. Totally in control, grinding me down, waiting for his moment. I always knew that the fight could play out like this. We discussed it in training, studied the scenario, made a game plan for it. I'm waiting too. A minute into the fifth, I get my chance.

Jackson hits me with an uppercut and chases me onto the ropes, those big rights coming in volleys of twos and threes. As I'm moving off to get away, I roll my ankle, but he doesn't see that. All he sees is me stumbling slightly, and it looks like a delayed reaction to his last shot. He misreads it and senses that he's only one clean punch away from putting the fight to bed. He steps in with an executioner's intent but he's slightly out of distance. I bend my legs, making him miss and at the same time creating an angle, and let my right hook go. It happens in a blink of an eye, so precise that the power is almost incidental. I don't need to look at the spoils of war; the referee doesn't need to count. He's out cold on the canvas, that lethal right arm of his trapped beneath his fallen body. Game over.

I hear him call it a lucky punch afterwards. It reveals more about him than it does about the shot. There's nothing lucky about the hours we've spent in the gym, Adam with the pad on his right hand, swiping it towards me, repeating the same set of instructions like a prayer. Bend your legs. Make him miss. Hook. Bend your legs. Make him miss. Hook. Over and over again. In the white heat of the ring, everything that we've been working on for the last two years – the head movement, how to fight up close – comes to me instinctively for the first time. He's putting it on me but there's no panic now, not like the Chávez fight. I know how to react and how to handle the pressure. Even though I'm under serious fire, I'm still punching and taking my head out, looking for angles and moving my head after every punch and dropping low after every punch, while his head is in one spot and he is offloading. That's what makes the difference. That's what helps me to survive that onslaught and land my shot. There's nothing lucky about hard work.

I don't need to be reminded what this win means. Lou DiBella, my promoter, is the first person in the ring to celebrate with us; he got me this fight. Now hopefully my career is back on track. Later that night, Adam stops me as I go to duck out the side door of the arena afterwards. 'Not tonight. You've just won that belt. Put it on and walk out with me.'

It reminds me of Emanuel. Everyone imagines that there's an incredible party on fight night, a red-carpet affair with guest lists and velvet ropes and DJs and bottle service. But when I'm done fighting, I just want to get out of there, get back to my room and totally unwind. Do nothing. Maybe get some room service. But I remember one night at the Orleans in Vegas when Emanuel insisted: 'Come on, we're walking out this way.'

A lot more people wanted to stop and talk to Emanuel than talk to me, but he was right to insist that night, and now Adam is too. You work so hard for your wins, make so many sacrifices, put yourself through the wringer for weeks, and you're so crushed when you lose, you have to savour those victories when they come. You never know when the next one will be; if there will be a next one. One punch won it for me tonight, and one punch could end it all just as quickly the next time. They're the stakes that we're playing with. So I put on my new NABF light-middleweight title belt and I follow Adam. We walk through the Garden to our seats just before the main event, Cotto v Martínez, is about to start. This time, I'm the one that people want to talk to.

'Lee, Lee, Lee.'

'Well done tonight, Andy. Great fight.'

'That knockout, man. What a punch.'

I'm stopped fifty, sixty times, easily, before we can get to our seats. Handshakes, photos, selfies, autographs, simple words of recognition and congratulations. After the fight too. Our hotel is only a block away from the arena, directly across the street, and it takes us the best part of an hour and a half to get out of Madison Square Garden and get back there. It's a long time since I've had this feeling. I'm in no rush.

‹ ›

The two sides of being a boxer, the person and the fighter, don't always go hand in hand.

Boxing, by its nature, is a lonesome pursuit. If you're lucky, you'll have a supportive team around you – your coach, your team-mates, your family, your friends – but you're the only one who can do the work. You're the only one who can put in the hard yards, day after day, in the gym or on the road. When you're training, you spend a lot of time in your own company, in your own head, planning, preparing, thinking. Once a fight is agreed and you're in camp, you cut yourself off from the outside world and its distractions. You become selfish. You have to. You put yourself and your needs front and centre in every decision. Is this going to benefit me in my preparation and in my fight? That's the only consideration that matters. And when the time comes for you to step into that ring, nobody else can throw a punch or dodge one for you. You're on your own and you have to do it all by yourself.

When those blinkers come on, you forget the simplest things. When I'm away in camp, I won't see Maud for weeks. When she rings, she'll ask me about my day, how I'm getting on, and I tell her, but sometimes it doesn't occur to me to ask about hers or see if she has any news from back home. That's the reality of a fighter's mind. You're conscious of this behaviour, of how self-centred it is, but it's hard to suppress it. It's not something that you can just switch on and off once a fight is over; it takes a while to decompress. I could sit down to have a meal with Maud a few days later and I'd be so used to being alone with my thoughts, that laser-like focus, that I'd sit there and eat almost in complete silence. She understands.

The people around you are the ones that you need the most, the ones that you latch on to most tightly, the ones to whom you are truly indebted. When I first moved to Detroit, I was just a boy. My family made sure that I always had someone there in the crowd – my mam, a lot of the time – as well as having Roger in my corner. Their support is so important to me. Over the years, I made a lot of good friends through my fights, people who I barely knew to begin with but who spent their time and money to follow me all over America, investing a serious amount in me and my career. All of these people, they only want to see you succeed because they know how badly you want it, how much the defeats hurt. They hurt as well. I lost some of these people along the way: Johnny, Daniel, and Emanuel. You do it for them as much as you do it for yourself.

There's a contradiction at the heart of being a boxer. When I move to London, I tell my family not to worry about coming to my first few fights with Adam, that it's no big deal, that I'll win. When the bigger fights come, that consciously becomes part of the way I like to do things. I feel that I have to totally detach myself to be at my best. They would always ask if I want them there, if I need them there, but I tell them that this is something I have to take care of by myself. It's hard to explain. I hope they understand.

‹ ›

I hope that Adam is calling with good news. And he is.

'Andy, it's done. We've got the fight.'

Adam's a genius. I don't know what strings he had to pull to make this happen, because my name should never have been in the mix. I'm not too concerned. I've a world title fight to prepare for.

It should have been so straightforward. Peter Quillin was WBO middleweight champion and set to make a mandatory defence against Matt Korobov, the number-one contender. Then it all got political. There was a purse bid for the fight – like a silent auction, where every promoter makes an offer and whoever puts up the most money wins the right to stage the fight. Golden Boy, Quillin's promoter, put in their bid; Top Rank, Korobov's promoter, put in their bid. But then there was a third bid from Roc Nation, the company owned by Jay-Z, that blew them both out of the water. They put up an insane amount of money, nearly $2 million, and as champion, Quillin was in line to get about three-quarters of that. But there's a long-running dispute between Quillin's manager, Al Haymon, and Jay-Z dating back to the time when Haymon was the manager of Destiny's Child. Quillin refused to fight on an event being run by Jay-Z, but the title defence had been ordered by the WBO, so if he didn't want to fight, the only other option was to vacate his title and surrender his belt.

The WBO accept a request to allow Demetrius Andrade, their light-middleweight champion, to move up a division and fight Korobov for the vacant title, but, for whatever reason, he passes. It sounds like good news for the next man in line, Billy Joe Saunders, but he's already got plans in place for a big all-English fight against Chris Eubank Jr, and he'd have to cancel that to take the Korobov fight.

Adam's watching all this like a hawk. I've no problem moving back up to middleweight if there's a title shot on the line. He rings Frank Warren, Saunders's promoter, to see if they can come to some sort of arrangement.

'They need someone for Korobov, and I think they'll agree to Andy. Can you move him in the ratings so that we can make the fight? And if he wins, Billy Joe gets the first shot when he defends it next year.'

Warren agrees. We have ourselves a deal.

———

I take my gloves off; I'm not sure if there's much point in putting them back on again. Everything in life – everything in a lot of people's lives – has been geared towards this. Not for a couple of weeks or months. For years. This is the shot. There ain't no second chances. Remember, Emanuel said it that night against Chávez. Well, you're getting a second chance here. You're the lucky one. Weeks out from a world title fight and you show up to training camp, first day of sparring, and you barely win a round. These lads you're in with are good, but you're supposed to be a world title contender. When all those people who never believed in you kept mouthing off, saying you were never as good as Emanuel thought, you insisted they were wrong, that they didn't know you like he did, that they didn't know what you were capable of. And now look at you. You're going to show up here for the next six weeks, waste your time, waste Adam's time, waste everyone's time. Spend a small fortune on the apartment, on the camp, on travel, on eating right, on getting everything right. Starve yourself half to death again. And then perform like that when it actually matters, when you actually have to get into the ring. What's the point? Maybe you should just call the whole thing off now while you can.

The first day of sparring is a bad one for me. The two boys I'm in with, Deion Jumah and John Ryder, are both young lads. Strong British prospects but a good few steps down from where I'm at. That's why they're here as the sparring partners and I'm here, supposedly, as a legitimate world title contender. You wouldn't know it to look at us in there. Between them, they push me around the floor for eight rounds; I win one. I know Adam's worried because he doesn't say much. He probably doesn't even know where to begin. If this is where we're starting from, we've a long way to go. I'm legitimately worried, worried enough that the thought of pulling out of the fight crosses my mind and I don't dismiss it immediately.

No two days of sparring are ever alike. Emanuel used to always say it to me, mainly because I was bossing my way through rounds and he was trying to keep me sharp and on my toes. You might get the better of someone today, but you better be ready tomorrow because they'll be coming for you and they'll want to prove a point. The shoe is on the other foot. Now I'm the one trying to show that anyone can have a bad day, that what happened in that first session was just a blip. I work hard on the pads with Adam, I listen to what he's telling me. When I get back in the ring with Deion and John the next time, I assert myself early, don't let them take control easily. Within a week, I'm dominating them.

It was Adam's suggestion to have the full camp in the south of France. It makes sense. Any of the times I've been to Monaco, visiting him and Claire and the family since they moved out to live here, the setup has always been as good as anything back in the UK. The gym he uses in Nice is up to scratch, and it's only half an hour down the road in the car. Perfect autumn weather too; about twenty degrees, not too warm, but far better than the cold and rain. When you're pushing yourself to the limit, the little things matter. 'Maud should come out and live here with you for the couple of months,' he suggests. 'It would do you the world of good to have her around.'

He takes me looking for an apartment and we find a beautiful one in Beausoleil, up on the hill, just across the border from Monaco. Maud will love it; she could live here forever with the high ceilings, the wooden floors, the balcony looking out over the beach, the short walk to the sea in the morning. She has just finished up a run of shows back in Dublin. The timing is perfect. In all of our years together, she has never really been around during my training camps. It's always been something that I've had to do by myself. A time for eating, a time for training, and a time for sleeping, latching onto the monotony of the routine like a comfort blanket.

Training isn't any easier but life is so much more relaxed because she's there, so much more normal, and normality, any semblance of it, is priceless when you're preparing for the biggest fight of your life. She looks after all of my meals, knows exactly what to make, in what quantity, and when to have it ready. She keeps me calm. Keeps me focused. She takes a little cardboard box out of her suitcase and hands it to me, tells me to keep it by our bed, have a look through it when I'm resting. It's a box of affirmation cards, positive messages and reflections. I read them every day.

There's a structure to everything we do. Richard Towers flies out for part of the camp, and Ryan Burnett comes out to help as well. I'm a changed fighter. I've kept my Kronk roots, but I finally feel comfortable in the style of fighting that Adam is teaching me. My body has adapted and I'm thriving on the training. They're hard, hard sessions but every day brings another little victory. Eight rounds of the leg circuit when I could only do six rounds a month ago. Ten rounds of the arm circuit that I couldn't do at all when I started out with Adam. A whole round of sparring where I'm just in full flow and Adam doesn't have to stop and correct me once.

'Yes, that's it, that's it. You're doing it now, you're doing it.'

And I push myself harder in the gym, and I walk by the boulangerie in the morning, ignoring the siren song of the fresh bread as it sits there cooling, denying myself, because it's all part of the sacrifice. Because I'm doing this for a purpose that means more to me than any pain I might have to go through, something that I want more than anything in the world.

Those hard sessions, getting through them and being able to go again the next day, it gives me belief. It hardens my resolve. It frees me to want something so badly and yet at the same time not be crushed by the pressure of wanting it so much – it allows me to walk that tightrope of emotions. The dread, the fears, the enormity of the consequences, they all dissipate in the face of hard work and perseverance. I remember the Bog Road. And when I go to bed at night, I know I'm doing more than anybody else. I know I'm training more than anybody else. Wherever Korobov is, he's not working as hard as me. He doesn't want this as much as I want it. He couldn't.

There's a church in Beausoleil. I've never prayed for something for myself, I never will again, but I go to mass every Sunday and I pray. Just let me win this fight, I pray. Just this one.

〈 〉

Every day I take out my notebook and pen and I write:

On December 13th I will become world champion.
On December 13th I will become world champion.
On December 13th I will become world champion.
On December 13th I will become world champion.
On December 13th I will become world champion.

I study those eight words, absorb their full meaning, and then I put the notebook away again.

———

Billy Walsh and Zaur Antia told me about Matt Korobov, the Russian who was cleaning up the middleweight division after I turned pro. As good as Gaydarbekov, who won the 2004 Olympic gold, maybe even better. Amateur world champion in 2005, and again in 2007. The more they saw of him, in camps, in tournaments, the more impressed they were. More than once, I'd come home to visit, stop in to say hello, and the conversation would turn to Korobov.

'Wait till you see this guy fight, Andy. You and him would have been a great fight. It would have been great to see you in against him.'

I've seen him fight a lot now. He's always on my mind. I know how good he is, I have the utmost respect for him, but I'm absolutely convinced that I can beat him. We're boxers, the two of us, and that will play to my strengths. I've been beaten in fights, outmuscled in fights, overpowered in fights, but nobody has ever managed to out-box me in a fight.

I have two losses on my record, 33–2, but Korobov is still unbeaten, 24–0 since he turned professional. Adam watches the tapes of some of his recent fights but there's nothing impressive or remarkable about the way he's boxing, the way he's winning. He turns them off, and switches on some old amateur tapes instead. We want to prepare for him at his best.

Everything has its place. An obsessive attention to detail. The Boxing Booth way. It's all coordinated, down to the clothes we're wearing. A team uniform. When I move to Adam, I start wearing black and red, a complete departure from Emanuel's insistence on light, bright colours, a sub-conscious statement. I wear a fox on the leg of my shorts now in tribute. Emanuel liked foxes because a fox is an animal that gets by on its wits and cleverness, not strength: the Detroit Fox was his nickname when he boxed. Adam wants everyone around me dressed in black T-shirts with the red BB logo. Black trousers. Luke arrives and doesn't have black runners with him. He runs across to the nearest shop and buys a pair. All black everything.

This is the level of organisation that Adam brings to fight week. He can't control what happens in the ring but he can control everything else up to that point. Nothing is left to chance from the moment we arrive. He flies a team out to Las Vegas to make sure that nothing gets missed: Dave Coldwell, Richard Towers, Terry Clark, Dave Nicolosi, our head of security. John Hill, the operations manager, has his clipboard with a checklist. Everybody has their role, knows where they have to be, what they have to do.

From the moment we step off the plane in McCarran, I'm already walking, talking, thinking like a champion. Emanuel and Sugar Hill, they always had their own style when it came to running fight week, but this is next-level professionalism. I used to watch enviously as fighters like Martínez came into a room with their support team, their entourage, and quietly commanded it with their presence and their authority. All he had to do was focus on the fight; everything else was someone else's responsibility. Now I know how it feels. When we go to the public workout, when we go to the press conference, we move in a pack.

Before his fight against Tommy Hearns in 1985, Marvin Hagler wore a red and white cap that simply said WAR. I get one made for myself, a black hat with red stitching. My new colours. A nod to Hagler. A statement of intent.

Maud arrives a few days later with Claire, Adam's wife, and the two of us are waiting to meet them when their taxi pulls up outside the hotel. We all spend Thursday night together, relaxing in our room, watching the boxing from California on ESPN. Johnathon Banks is fighting in the co-main against Antonio Tarver, and Sugar Hill is there in his corner. The whole card is dull and Adam sits there, half-watching, half-listening to me as I pick apart the flaws. I'm relaxed, not preoccupied or distracted, fully dialled in to what I'm looking at, the poor performances we're being forced to endure. When we finished our final workout, Adam told me that I looked like a world champion but, he tells me later, sitting there watching TV, that's the moment he was certain that I was ready.

Maud makes breakfast on the morning of the fight. We eat together, she gives me a kiss goodbye, wishes me luck, and leaves me to relax and get ready. I lie on the bed and flick on the television. I leave it on the Discovery Channel for the entire day, watching episodes of *How It's Made* until it's time to leave to go to the arena.

Adam and Claire are at breakfast when Maud comes down to the dining room. She sits with them and the nerves finally hit; they manifest themselves as tears. This, today, this is what it has all been for. I can't allow myself to reflect on that journey, but she can, and the thought of it is overwhelming. The next time she sees me, I'll be world champion or it will all be over. For my sake, for no other reason, she is desperate for it to be the former. Adam assures her that it will be. 'I don't think he will win. I expect him to win.'

There's no trace of doubt, no hint of ambiguity. He is scientific in his certainty: we have a plan; Andy knows it, Andy will execute it, and Andy will win.

I think about the plan as I lie there. We've broken it down to its most basic, the bullet points. No sense in over-complicating things now. Keep your shoulders loose. Keep stepping the feet. Take the distance. And flow. That's the plan.

Flow; engage the subconscious brain, in other words. Don't be rash or reckless, but don't paralyse yourself with possibility either. Feel the fight as it unfolds in front of you and fight it.

———

Flow. I call timeout on a sparring session so that I can speak to Adam. It's a couple of weeks out from the fight against Jackson, and things are finally starting to click in our partnership. A sixth sense of how each other likes to do things, and finding the balance that works for us. I'm comfortable telling Adam what works for me and what doesn't, and he's comfortable listening to what I'm saying. This isn't working. I'm in there against a really tough opponent, Sergei, and I'm struggling. Adam's making it harder, not easier. He's very vocal, breaking down my performance, trying to feed me instructions and information in real time. It's impossible to focus. My mind is juggling too many pieces of information at once: what I'm seeing in front me, how I'm reacting, and then Adam's perspective on the fight and what he's trying to steer me towards as well. In the end, it's all coming out in a disjointed muddle and I can't get to grips with this guy at all.

'Adam, listen, for this round just say nothing. Just let me box and don't say anything.'

We box a couple of rounds and Adam watches on in silence. It's a completely different spar. I start to fight instinctively, and with much better results. When we're done, Adam is curious as to why the silence made so much of a difference.

'Why did you ask me to do that?'

'Because by the time you say something to me and I process it and then try to execute it, the moment's gone. You might have seen it, I might have seen it, but it's gone. The subconscious mind sees things so much quicker than the conscious mind. You know, just let me flow.'

———

The mood in the dressing room is as light as ever. That sense of preparedness has become a sense of readiness. All week, I've been seeing signs around me, the circle completing itself. Everything has a familiar feel. Kenny Bayless, the referee, comes in to give me his final instructions. Even Kenny, what he's saying to me now, it's familiar. He refereed me the night I beat Ortega, the night Johnny was on my shoulder, throwing those last punches with me.

I watch the undercard fights with the sound turned down, my music playing instead. Disco, funk, soul. Dancing music. Stevie Wonder. Aretha Franklin. The classics. Forgotten cuts from deep in the Motown vault that I stumbled across once and then kept forever. I stay loose. Richard comes in, holds out his hands and gets me to throw a few punches in twos and threes, find that snap-snap-snap rhythm. We do that for a couple of minutes and then I go back to stretching and rolling. I'm ready, not impatient.

And then the time comes. When I get to the ring, as myself and Korobov feel each other out in those opening rounds, I'm very conscious of where I am, very aware of my surroundings. I can hear the commentary from the HBO judge at ringside, marking the early rounds for Korobov because he's been a little bit busier. I know there's a strong Irish crowd there. Their encouragement, their energy lifts me when Korobov gets the better of an exchange, wins a little moment. I can pick Maud's voice out so clearly that I know where in the crowd she is: over near Adam, somewhere to the right of our corner. I can hear her nerves. I tune it all out. Clear my head. Focus.

Korobov shades the first couple of rounds. He's doesn't have to do much to win them. It's cagey, but he's marginally more composed, feeling his way into the fight a bit quicker than I am. Adam tries to keep me calm, not let me get frustrated. There's not a lot in it.

'Remember. Shoulders loose. Keep stepping the feet. Keep doing what you're doing. It's good, it's good.'

I'm too eager when my chance comes in the third round, my first real opportunity to test Korobov and see if he stands up. I land a left hand and I jump on him. I force my punches, no precision or accuracy, and he's able to bat them away. Adam gets me back on the stool at the bell and reminds me to be patient. We spoke about this.

'Don't panic. You went too quick there. It will come. Take your time.'

He's tricky, moving well, making it hard for me to hit him. I try to work behind my jab, but I'm either too far away or getting in too close. I still haven't found the right range, haven't settled into a rhythm where I can throw in quick twos and threes that will hurt him. Another round slips between my fingers, and another.

Adam's right. There's no need to take risks. If I've to hang tough and take him into the last rounds, so be it. I'll die on my shield here before I lose on points. I'll wear him down. Tired fighters make mistakes. Tired fighters leave themselves exposed. If I get the right chance, I'll only need one shot.

We size each other up in the sixth. He feints a jab and I bite, take half a step back to get myself out of harm's way for whatever he's got planned next. I step back in, fake to the body and then close the distance behind a straight left. Korobov's quick. He dips underneath it, making me miss again. We come together in a half-clinch, our bodies tangled for a beat, and as we push apart, he slams me with a short left hand that lands on the temple. I roll out and come up from underneath him as he swipes, just missing, with his right. I can't let him win this moment. I dig in to stand my ground and cancel him out if nothing else. I let my right hook go, my knockout punch, lashing out with spite and menace. It comes at him awkwardly, the kind of shot you can't brace yourself to take. He never sees it and that's what does the damage.

A gasp ripples through the building. I know he's hurt. I think he's gone. Like Daniels, like Jackson. I take a step back, ready to walk off as world champion, my arm held high in celebration. It lifts him off his feet, he staggers backwards, but he doesn't go down.

I get to him as fast as I can, while he's wobbling, unsteady, uncertain, and I let go. I'll never have this chance again. Time doesn't slow down like it does in the movies. My life, my career, doesn't flash before my eyes. I don't think of Repton, or Limerick, or the Kronk, or Emanuel or Adam or Maud. I don't dwell on those moments when the weight of this dream nearly broke me, and I found it in myself to push back from the brink and go again. I think about the punch I'm throwing, and the next one, and the next one. I reject emotion, embrace serenity. Calm, cool-headed precision.

I throw them hard. I throw them to hurt him. It's all measured. I've no idea how long is left in the round, but if I only have seconds, I have to make them count. I can't allow him to cover up, to survive. So I let the punches rain. Left uppercut. Right-left to the head. I plot, I move, I stalk my way around him like a vulture. Right to the body. Left-right-left to the head. He keeps his gloves up but I find my way through. Right uppercut. He stands there, surrenders to this savage frenzy. Right-left-right to the head. He's not moving, not even attempting to swing back, just covering up, covering up, but he won't go down. Another uppercut. I can't ease off. Left. Right. I can see the referee on my shoulder, hovering, eyes locked on Korobov. Jump in, jump in and stop this, jump in and wave it off. I pause and then unload another barrage. Jump in now. Now. Now.

Now I'm the champion of the world. The violence, the anger, the aggression all ceases in an instant, swept from the room by the roar of the crowd, replaced by pure elation. I've seen this moment a thousand times in my head, visualised how it would feel to watch the count hit ten or to be pushed away by the referee, and finally understand the beauty that life can be one way in that moment, and in the very next will never be the same again. You win belts and you lose belts, but once you're a champion, you're a champion forever.

I run to the corner and leap up onto the ropes, staring through the lights to find Maud. I see her, her red dress, pushing her way along the row of stunned Russian fans to try to get to me. Adam lifts me, presents me to the world. When he puts me down again, Maud is there, tearful, ecstatic. I don't even begin to explain how much I love her. I know this means as much to her as it does to me. She's been with me on this journey every step of the way. We've done it together.

They call the result, put my belt around my waist. Make it all official. Make it all surreal again.

The end comes at one minute and ten seconds of round number six. The winner, by TKO victory, and now the WBO middleweight champion of the world ...

Max Kellerman pulls me aside for an interview. I've prepared these words in so many idle moments, tying the laces on my boots, waiting for the kettle to boil. I start by thanking Adam. A thank you seems woefully inadequate. The impact that this man has had on my life in such a short space of time. We've only known each other for a little more than two years. Two years that felt like an eternity at times, two years when I was often at my lowest, but he had faith in me and never wavered, promised me that the top of the mountain wasn't as far away as it seemed, assured me that my patience and perseverance would be rewarded.

I hope Emanuel is watching me and smiling. I truly believe that he is, his prophecy finally fulfilled. I don't need a microphone to explain the debt that I owe him. That much is obvious without words. He gave me everything. I've repaid him now in the only way that I could ever begin to, the only way that he would have ever wanted. I've added one final name to his long list of champions. I've made his words come true.

The rest of the night passes in a blur, as life's best moments tend to do. There is no elaborate celebration, no wild party. Simple. Beautiful. Time spent savouring this occasion with the people who matter most to me. Nobody has anything else to do, any place else to be. I catch myself sitting there for a few minutes, a quiet observer at my own party, the tiredness hitting but the satisfaction, the giddiness, holding it at bay. Maud is a picture of pure happiness.

'You did it, babe. You did it.'

'I knew I was going to do it. I knew it.'

The night is still young and we stay there, sitting in the dressing room for what seems like hours. Marie Steward, Emanuel's wife, finds her way to us in the back of the arena and joins us to celebrate. She insisted on flying down from Detroit so that she could be here in person. I thank her for coming, tell her what a privilege it is to have her here with us, how deeply I appreciate it.

'I'm happy for you. I'm happy for you. You did it.'

She's seen it all a million times before, but it doesn't make this one any less special.

When the time comes to leave and move on somewhere else, Adam rounds people up. There's a huge crowd in the foyer of the hotel, waiting; so many friends, those people who have followed me throughout my whole career. John Carey, whom I met very early in my time in Detroit, is there with his wife Maggie. A group of my Irish friends that live in America: Seamus Fairclough, Darryl Doyle, Kevin Mahon. Another close friend, Pat Hartigan, tells me that he had a big bet on me to win. I was the 6/1 underdog to beat Korobov, and Pat has won more money than I made from the fight. Terry Cox from Mayo is there too, another person who has supported me through thick and thin. Terry was living in Chicago when I first met him. He came to see one of my early fights against a guy called James Morrow in 2007 and introduced himself afterwards and we became friends. Terry must have called me every day since then, just to say hello and see how I was getting on in training, if I had any plans for fights coming up. He travelled everywhere to see me. Of course he wouldn't miss this one tonight. When I see all of these faces, it is truly humbling. I'm so lucky to have these good people in my life, so fortunate to be able to give them a night like this.

Roy Jones Jr is one of the first people to stop me in the foyer. My boxing idol. The first gift Maud ever bought me when we started going out was a framed photo of Roy Jones Jr. And I remember standing just a few hundred metres down the road in 2004, on my first ever trip to Vegas with Emanuel, spotting him and waiting while he finished the conversation he was having. He had to rush off before I could get a photo that day, and now he's coming over to congratulate me.

'Andy, that right hook, man. You're a great fighter. Congratulations, champ.'

In among the hundreds of messages on my phone, there's one from Wladimir to congratulate me. I send him back a selfie, me holding up the belt, my prize. I finally got one, Wladimir.

It will be a few more days before I can celebrate with my family. They've been there on the good nights and the not so good, but this time they leave me to concentrate on getting the job done, and what will be will be. Bring the belt back home to them.

I had asked Roger if he wanted to be in the corner. He was there to help Adam in my first couple of fights but he was never consistently involved once we came back from Detroit. Now's not the time to change things again.

'No, Andy, I'll get too nervous. I'll just leave you to it.'

I knew what he meant. For years, he was my biggest strength in the final few hours before I stepped into the ring. We'd look at each other in the dressing room and I would immediately grow in confidence and in energy. But I could always tell when he was worried, and as the big brother, I'd try to reassure him: I've got this, it's all under control, don't worry. I can't even begin to imagine how hard it was for him to keep his emotions in check when I was in the thick of those wars, and then it played on my mind too. I would think about him and I would start to get emotional. He made the right call; I'd have to do this one by myself.

They're the first people we go to visit when we arrive back in London. We take Adam's car and we drive over to Romford to see him and my dad and Hayley and some of my cousins. We bump into an old friend of Ned's, Maurice Black, on the way and pull over onto the hard shoulder of the M25 and stop to take a picture: me, him, and the world title.

When we get to the site, there's more handshakes and hugs and photos. I ask Roger what he thought of the fight, where he watched it. He couldn't face being around a crowd to watch it live on Saturday night so he sat by himself in the trailer and watched it on a stream. Halfway through, as Korobov was putting the squeeze on, his stream died. Roger sprinted up the site in his underpants to a friend's trailer where they'd ordered the fight in for everyone to watch together. When he got there, it was over.

'What's going on with the fight? What's going on?'

'He's won, he's won, he's won.'

I see how much it means to my dad. He'll wear this proudly: his son, the world champion. The first Irishman to win a world title fight in America since Jimmy McLarnin in 1934. The first gypsy ever to become a professional world champion. The embarrassment that I used to feel coming back here, the worry about where my life was going, what people thought of me, it's all gone. The young lads still have their fancy cars; I have a world title that no money in the world can buy.

We fly back to Ireland the next day. The fire engines come out to escort us in from the runway in Shannon Airport, firing their water cannons into the air and making a rainbow to greet us as we land. My mam is there, waiting for me at the bottom of the steps when the door of the plane opens. Waiting for me to come home again.

It's all ahead of me over the next few days, memories to treasure for a lifetime, but first, we'll enjoy tonight. We go to

Adam's room where everyone has gathered to celebrate, but after a while, I slip away quietly with Maud and we go back to our room. I lie beside her in bed without sleeping, and I think about the road that we've travelled together and I doze and I smile.

EPILOGUE: DUBLIN

It's said that Napoleon was a great general because he convinced his men to risk death and glory on the battlefield rather than carry on their mundane lives in fields and factories.

For the best part of thirty-four years, boxing was where I found my reason to live. It was the path which allowed me to be somebody, my purpose when I had none. It challenged me to be great: to sacrifice in the pursuit of excellence, to risk in the hope of glory, to chase dreams that only the few can achieve. To persevere in the face of all adversity.

Boxing taught me more about myself than I could have ever learned elsewhere. You don't know who you are until you're in a fight. It remains the most pure test of character that there is; there is nothing like it. There's a level of self-examination, of self-discovery, in the months and weeks and days leading up to a fight. When the going gets tough, that's when your true self is revealed: your heart, your courage, your will.

Humans have fought for two hundred thousand years or more, the entirety of the history of the species. It was once the building block of society: you fought and you tested yourself and, if you lived, you knew where you stood. Your fighting prowess, your ability to attack, defend, and protect, was the most fundamental part of your identity. That kind of test no longer exists in the modern human experience, apart from at its extremities: on the battlefield, or in prison. There is no equivalent arena in which we can learn so much about who we are. Sport is the closest mirror that we have to hold up in front of us and see the essence of ourselves, our resilience and our frailty. Fighting, boxing, takes a magnifying glass to that image. There is no test like it left in the world.

I loved boxing. I loved training and pushing myself to the limit and coming out the other side a better person for having done it. I loved the toughness and the skill. I loved winning and all of the by-products that came with it, the recognition and the validation that it gave me.

When I decided to retire in February 2018, I was asked how I would like to be remembered. As an honest boxer, I answered; as a boxer who gave it my all, who never backed down from a fight. The night that I became world champion in December 2014, I promised that I would defend my belt and fight against the best in the world. I was never in any doubt that that was what I wanted to do. That's what a real fighter does. That's what a champion does. I was true to my word. As champion I fought two of the top middleweights in the world: a thrilling draw against the unbeaten Peter Quillin in April 2015, although that bout was ultimately a non-title fight, and then a decision defeat on two cards against Billy Joe Saunders in Manchester the following December.

When you lose in boxing, it's not like losing in any other sport. It's not a game of tennis, it's not a game of ping-pong. You're being dominated by another man, taking a physical beating at his hands while hundreds of thousands, if not millions, of people watch. The defeat on your record lasts forever but the embarrassment, the shame, they live with you for a long time as well. There was a guy, Dennis Turner, from the Kronk, who was involved around a few of my fights to look after the logistics and administration. In the days after the Chávez fight, he was around a lot, doing bits and pieces but mainly checking up on me.

'Andy, it's OK to look me in the eye.'

'What?'

'You can look me in the eye. Hold your head up, you can look me in the eye.'

I didn't even realise that I was doing it, but I hadn't looked him in the eye since I lost.

In the build-up to the Saunders fight, I made the mistake of allowing it to feel like more than just another fight. I had never fought against another gypsy before as a professional and I allowed the talk and the headlines to get to me. I knew it was being hyped up as a big fight among the gypsy community. I put more pressure on myself than I needed to. I told myself that there was more at stake, that there was more pride on the line against Saunders than there would be against any other fighter. I could see that my brothers were more invested in this fight than they would have been if it was a title defence against a different opponent. The gypsy community is small, and nearly everyone knows everyone. I wanted to win it for them so that they could say, 'Andy won, we told you he could beat that guy.'

The fight was cancelled twice, pushed back, rescheduled, moved from Limerick to Manchester with a never-ending series of press conferences, and when the time came to actually fight, I just wanted it to be over. I wasn't up for the fight or excited about it; I was sick of it. I was over-trained, burnt out, and being in a ring, or even being in the gym for training, was the last place I wanted to be. In the dressing room on the night of the fight, my legs felt like lead, weighed down with heaviness. I didn't say it to anyone, didn't even tell Adam, because I didn't want to make an issue out of it. But once I acknowledged it myself and started thinking about it, I gave it power. I tried to convince myself that I'd feel better once I got into the ring and started fighting, but I didn't pick up. I went looking for the easy way out by trying to hurt Saunders early, and in doing so I left myself open. I was impatient. I started chasing big shots, throwing recklessly and leaving my chin exposed. My power was my own worst enemy that night, and I lost to a good fighter.

A few weeks beforehand, I had watched Danny Jacobs defend his WBA title against Quillin, a huge fight between two more of the outstanding middleweights at the time. Jacobs stunned him with a flash knockdown in the first round, and I was watching Quillin thinking, hold him, hold him, hold him. There was a long time to go in the round, but if he'd held on to Jacobs, I'm sure he would have survived the round, and if he'd survived the round, who knows what would have happened with the rest of the fight. But he didn't. He chose to fight, and Jacobs finished him off.

That fight, just a fortnight earlier, was fresh in my memory when Saunders put me down in the third round. I was unsteady getting back to my feet but I knew exactly what I wanted to do. What took a few seconds seemed like an eternity. Just hold him, I thought. But when Saunders got to within about three feet of me, my scrambled mind wiped that common sense out the window and instead said, 'No, let him have it.' I started firing shots at him instead, and within ten seconds, he had dropped me again. It was a 10–7 round for Saunders, and it cost me my world title.

I couldn't be alone with my thoughts for a long time after that fight. It was very hard for me to sit by myself because eventually I'd start thinking about the fight and it was tearing me up. My phone was hardly ever out of my hand because I needed the distraction. I couldn't sleep at night. I had to listen to a podcast to occupy my mind until I fell asleep; now it has become a habit. I became obsessed with *Game of Thrones*: the books, the series, the recap videos, the fan sites, the conspiracy theories, whatever I could get my hands on. I just wanted to be anywhere except in real life and in the moment.

I loved boxing, but I was under no illusions. I knew how dangerous it was, how lethal it could be. But throughout my career, I never once considered the possibility that I might get hurt. It's like crossing the road. You know that people get knocked down and seriously injured when they cross the road, and you always exercise due caution, but you cross the road dozens of times a day without ever dwelling on the danger. You just don't think about it. You know it happens, but it won't happen to you.

The injuries, they're all little warnings, and they accumulate. When the end was coming near, I had to be honest with myself. In my first eight years as a pro, I had never so much as been knocked down once, but then between three fights in the space of eighteen months, I was on the canvas five times, and I had no desire to push my luck. Quillin was the hardest puncher I'd ever faced. One of his knockdowns should have been ruled a slip – he stood on my foot and the referee, Steve Willis, apologised to me afterwards – but the first time he caught me with that bomb of a right hook in the opening round, he hurt me. I don't remember any of the fight until the eleventh round. As I was getting up off the stool, I asked Adam how I was doing.

'What's going on? Should I go all out to knock him out?'

'No, just keep boxing him. You're in the fight.'

Adam was right. I was right there in it. I won the eleventh round but lost the last and the fight finished as a split draw. But I was so dazed by Quillin's shot that I hardly knew where I was.

Two weeks, maybe three weeks, before I fought Saunders, I went for my usual evening run around Adam's neighbourhood. As I was running, I looked up, and in the corner of my right eye, I saw a flash, bright yellow, in my peripheral vision. I looked again and it happened again. And then I started noticing it any time I looked left or right sharply. When I got back home, I didn't mention it to anyone. Didn't tell Adam, didn't want any fuss, so I just kept it to myself and went ahead and fought. Eventually I mentioned it to Maud when we were back in Dublin a few weeks later.

'That shouldn't be happening. You've got to go and get it checked out.'

'It'll be grand. I'm sure it'll be fine in a week or two.'

'And what if it's not fine? Go and get it checked.'

She knew I wouldn't, so she made the appointment herself for me. When I did go, our GP was concerned enough to refer me to Paul Connell, a consultant in the Mater Hospital. As soon as he checked it out, he was concerned.

'OK, you've got a detachment in the retina of your right eye. I've just spoken to my colleague and you're very lucky because we've just had an opening at three o'clock and we can operate on you today.'

I called Maud to tell her. She was in the car, halfway down the country with her mam and Zoe, heading off on a trip they had booked as a Christmas present.

'What? You're having the operation now? Today?'

'Yeah, they can do it today so I'm going to get it done and get it over with. It's grand.'

David Keegan, a specialist, did the operation that afternoon, and when I woke up, Maud was there at my bedside. As soon as she'd hung up the phone, she turned the car around.

That was the final twist of the knife from the Saunders defeat, the last sickening little kick when I was already down: I lost my world title fighting with a detached retina. It happened around the time that I noticed it, two or three weeks out, a punch in sparring that did more damage than I realised. I had got my eyes tested when the fight was originally scheduled for September. Had I got them tested again, the fight would have been cancelled – for a third time – I would have been out of action for six or seven months after the surgery, and it's quite possible that the two of us would never have fought. But like all of the ups and downs throughout my career, even if they caused me worry and frustration and hurt at the time, I believe that they happened for a reason. I am who I am today because of all these things.

A few months after the Saunders fight, the stakes changed. Life changed. And boxing quickly became a risk that I wasn't willing to take any more. Maud and I became the most proud parents in the summer of 2017 when Julia, our daughter, was born. I got back into the ring one last time in March 2017, a few months before Julia arrived, and finished my career on a winning note with a victory over KeAndrae Leatherwood: win number thirty-five to go alongside the three defeats and a draw. I barely took a punch that night as I coasted to a points win. I could have pushed myself, went after the knockout, but it wasn't worth putting myself in harm's way. Even then, Julia was on my mind.

When the time came to retire, it was an easy decision to make. I kept training right up until the end, stayed in shape, stayed ready. There were offers of fights on the table, but when I weighed them up, there was nothing big enough or significant enough to convince me that I wanted to leave my home, my wife, and my child for twelve or fourteen weeks to go back into a training camp.

Around the time when I finally decided to call it quits – and announced the decision, so that there could be no turning back – we watched the film *Journeyman*. It's the story of a world middleweight champion with a beautiful wife and a baby daughter. He takes a blow to the head in his final title defence before retirement and ends up with a serious injury. This fictional character, Matty Burton, his story was so close to mine, so eerily close, and an insight into how my life maybe could have turned out if I had gone back and kept on fighting. I cried that night watching it, the first time I cried in years. It hammered home how lucky I am to have had a good career, and a good life so far. My only priority now is to take care of Maud and Julia, and not have them taking care of me.

It's hard sometimes to weigh up how finely life is balanced, how it sits on this knife edge where one punch can change everything. How your entire life – your health, your happiness, your career – is bound up in these decisions that you make every second that you're in the ring. It's hard to know why a life turns out the way it does. Maybe you make your own fate. Maybe it's your destiny.

ACKNOWLEDGEMENTS

I would like to thank everybody who helped bring this book together: to Ciarán Medlar who has supported the project from the very first day, and to all at BDO Ireland; to Damian McCann who, as always, was there for me whenever I needed him; to Niall Kelly for his help; and to the entire team at Gill Books, especially Conor Nagle, Catherine Gough, Ellen Monnelly and Sarah McCoy. Thank you all.

– Andy